PLANT PORTRAITS

Beth Chatto

PLANT PORTRAITS

Beth Chatto

*with colour paintings and pencil drawings by Jill Coombs
and line drawings by Christine Grey-Wilson*

J.M. Dent & Sons Ltd
London & Melbourne
In association with the Telegraph Sunday Magazine

First published 1985
© The Sunday Telegraph Ltd. 1985

This book is set in 10/11½ Apollo by Jolly & Barber Ltd, Rugby
Printed in Italy by Sagdos SPA, Milan, for
J.M. Dent & Sons Ltd
Aldine House, 33 Welbeck Street, London W1M 8LX

British Library Cataloguing in Publication Data

Chatto, Beth
    Plant portraits.
    1. Plants, ornamental
    I Title
    635   SB406

    ISBN 0-460-04600-4

PREFACE

This collection of plant portraits originated when I was asked by the editor of the Sunday Telegraph colour supplement to write a plant portrait for each Sunday of the year. I did so for two years.

They are not my hundred and four favourite plants, but just a few of the hundreds of favourite plants I have in my garden. I love all my plants for different reasons. Each year I see them reappear my pleasure in growing them is re-kindled and I feel the urge to try to capture them in words.

In winter the choice is limited, but by early spring there is a handful to choose from every week, while midsummer provides basketsful of flowers and foliage, both large and small, flamboyant or modest, all needed for the part they play in creating a garden.

The enthusiasm for uncommon plants has become widespread in recent years so I knew many readers would recognize and enjoy old friends among my portraits. But I hope that other readers, who may not yet have discovered some of these plants, will be inspired to try something different in their gardens. Whether you are a beginner, or a connoisseur of plants, the thrill of growing a new plant is just as keen.

The original drawings for the Telegraph Sunday Magazine were made by Joy Simpson and were much enjoyed and appreciated by many readers who kept them, as I have done, pasted into an album. I should like to take this opportunity to say thank you to all those readers who so kindly wrote to tell me that they had enjoyed the Plant Portraits. I also received many letters asking where the plants could be obtained. While some are being offered in garden centres, and by small adventurous nurseries, others may still be elusive. Apart from trees and shrubs my nursery can usually offer most of them.

When it was suggested that Plant Portraits might be published in book form a few alterations were made. I was asked to enlarge each article to fit the new space. During the first writing I often had to prune and discard details I would have liked to keep, so it became an interesting exercise in writing to expand the pieces without letting the seams show too obviously.

An opportunity was also given for the the talented work of two new artists to be exhibited. Jill Coombs and Christine Grey-Wilson have both gone to great lengths to paint or draw each plant from life. Christine has a house not too far away from my garden so could make occasional trips to find the odd plants she needed. She proves with her clean and elegant line drawings that beauty in plants, as in people, is not skin deep, but depends on fine form and modelling. Jill had to make longer journeys so on one trip I had the pleasure of her staying with me and could see the intensity of effort as well as the time and patience needed to re-create the brilliance of petals, or texture of leaves.

Some may ask, why write plant portraits or paint them when colour photography is so good? There is not a simple answer. But each of us who has contributed to this book has lived with these plants in our hands. We have each seen them differently, tried to express it, and then share it with you.

Beth Chatto

Spring 1985

The Beth Chatto Gardens and Nursery are open to the public from 9 am to 5 pm from March to mid-November (Monday to Saturday) and from mid-November to February (Monday to Friday). They are not open on Sundays or bank holidays, and are closed for two weeks during the Christmas recess.

A fully descriptive catalogue is available, but Beth Chatto regrets plants cannot be exported to the USA and Canada. Please write for current price to:

'Unusual Plants'
The Beth Chatto Gardens
Elmstead Market
Colchester, Essex C07 7DB
Telephone: Wivenhoe (020 622) 2007

Viburnum × *bodnantense*

Winter Flowering Viburnums

Now that the trees stand bare and bony, and the last chrysanthemums look sad and bedraggled, it is refreshing to catch the sweet scent of *Viburnum farreri*, better known as *Viburnum fragrans*, and to see its clusters of narrow tubular white flowers which open from deep rosy buds. The main display is usually before Christmas, in a spell of reasonably mild weather, but although frost browns the opened flowers the closed buds will survive, and continue to open intermittently until the spring. They are carried on thin leafless branches hanging gracefully from the main support stems which shoot up straight from the base to about 5 or 6 ft. These stout stems are warm chestnut-brown when young, with ragged bark.

An old shrub can become rather tangled, and is improved if occasionally some of the oldest stems are cut out from the base, and some of the upper brushwood is trimmed out as well. This encourages fresh branches which are wreathed with finer sprays of flower.

I also have the hybrid called *Viburnum* × *bodnantense*. It is similar, but has slightly bolder clusters of flower with warmer carmine-rose tinting. It is just as sweetly scented but, being of stouter habit, the flower clusters are held on straighter, stiffer branches so that they do not have quite the delicate curving charm of *V. farreri* when I am looking for a few branches to bring indoors. When cut they last longer in rooms without central heating. Like many winter flowers they soon drop in a warm dry atmosphere.

An advantage of *V.* × *bodnantense* is that its flowers seem to be more frost resistant than those of *V. farreri*, so apart from exceptionally severe winters, the whole bush creates a spring-like scene, very heartening to come across on gloomy winter days. To add to the feeling of life and warmth it would help to surround the bushes with a few clumps of *Tellima grandiflora* 'Rubra', or perhaps some of the new and improved forms of *Bergenia* whose leaves assume such vivid tints, bright carmine-red and dark polished purple, when grown in exposed positions.

I think it helps in garden design, if you can, to group together plants which are contributing something at the same time, rather than scattering them like confetti. I am thinking of aconites under *Hamamelis mollis*, or a group of *Helleborus niger*, faintly flushed with pink, which flower beneath my winter flowering cherry, *Prunus subhirtella* 'Autumnalis Rosea'.

Viburnums need a stiff moisture-retentive soil and will show distress if allowed to suffer from drought, but they also need plenty of sunlight to produce flowers abundantly.

Polygonum affine

The over-wintering habit of this late-summer flowering Knotweed is so attractive that it frequently catches my eye in January where it makes a glowing carpet along the edge of one of my damp borders. In summer its densely packed creeping shoots are set with narrow, dark green leaves. From early July to October a succession of 6-inch stems topped with spikes of little shrimp-pink flowers makes a pretty display. Another form I have, called 'Superbum', commences with almost white flowers which deepen to pink and finally mature to deep raspberry red, all stages being present on the same stretch of 'carpet'. (I have picked these dainty spikes of mature flowers and hung them upside down to dry in a warm room. They retain much of their shape and colour to add to winter decorations.)

With the onset of winter and frosty nights the leaves do not drop off, but remaining shapely they turn deep reddish-brown, a lovely, lively colour, making vivid contrast with the emerald-green mown grass when lit by winter sunlight. If you bend down and look closely you will see that these old but decorative leaves are partially sheltering the new young leaves already formed and clustered in the base of the stems, or on the ends of adventuring shoots.

Polygonum affine 'Donald Lowndes' has shorter spikes of seemingly double flowers, of a uniform shade of salmon pink. They create a good effect, but so far I have not found this plant such an enthusiastic grower as my other forms of *P. affine*. It tends to die out in patches, to need replanting and cosseting a little, but I am prepared to take the trouble since it has a special charm.

Another very pretty, creeping *Polygonum* is *P. vacciniifolium*. Its leaves disappear completely in winter leaving a fine web of warm rusty-brown stems to drape over any surface, whether paving, steps, or edge of border. Tiny leaves appear in spring to create a fresh green carpet until late summer and autumn when it is smothered for weeks with short slender spires of tiny pink flowers.

These polygonums will grow in sun provided they have soil which does not dry out. *P. affine*, for instance, will grow almost anywhere in reasonably moisture-retentive soil. They flower best in full sun where they also make excellent ground-cover. They can also be used as cover plants in part shade but there will be fewer flowers.

Polygonum affine

Betula jacquemontii

An Unusual Birch

There is scarcely a more graceful tree than our own native Silver Birch, *Betula pendula*, but there is another, with much smoother, more brilliantly white stems and branches, which comes from the mountain forests of Nepal, in the Himalayas. It is called *Betula jacquemontii*. To stand close to its trunk on a clear sunny day in winter, with blue sky above, and look up into the wide spread of seemingly white-washed branches culminating in a tracery of fine twigs, is a marvellous experience. The bark, which covers the main framework, is ivory-white, smooth and thin like writing paper.

In fanciful mood I imagine the wide papery strips which peel off in layers like sheets from a manuscript book complete with faint brown lines of varying widths, being used by a musician or poet to write a special message, perhaps a line of melody or a valentine.

On dark winter afternoons my eye is caught by its perfect shape, a delicate ivory fan outlined against the black bulk of holly that stands some way beyond it. My tree stands alone in mown grass, reflecting itself like a swan in a small, dark-surfaced pool.

Although they are very desirable, birches have greedy surface-seeking roots which starve the soil for many plants beneath them. *B. jacquemontii* eventually makes a more robust tree than our native birch, with larger leaves. It looks best isolated but can be enjoyed as part of a shrubbery where its gleaming branches can be seen high overhead.

Another lovely birch, a selected form of *B. pendula*, is the Swedish cut-leafed birch, generally known as *B. p.* 'Dalecarlica'. It eventually makes a tall slender tree with drooping branches and small diamond-shaped leaves with deeply serrated edges. It is a particularly pretty tree to use as a specimen in a lawn, or better still, if there is room, to plant a little grove of them in grass, where you can walk close to enjoy the lacy effect of twigs and leaves.

Betula ermanii is another I like very much when a well-grown tree shows off a creamy tinted trunk and warm orange-brown branches, while the famous American birch, *B. papyrifera*, the 'Canoe' or 'Paper Birch', makes a large tree with white papery bark. It also contributes to autumn with handsome yellow foliage.

There are many other birches. It is worth a trip to a good arboretum to see mature specimens.

Birches can be grown on most soils, both damp and dry, but will not do so well on shallow chalk soils.

Winter Jasmine

At no time of year I think do we grow a shrub or climber more beautiful than winter jasmine (*Jasminum nudiflorum*) when at its best. To suddenly come upon a shower of green leafless stems studded with yellow can take your breath away when all around looks chilled and lifeless.

A little care and effort is needed to produce the best effect. Where there is room it can be left to sprawl over a bank, but generally it is planted against a wall. One of the easiest and least noticeable ways to support it is to drill the wall and insert vine-eyes which you can buy at hardware shops. Then make a framework of stout covered wire, old telephone wire is ideal. Once you have grown the jasmine to cover your support try to remember to prune it after flowering. Cut out the flowered shoots, and old twiggy pieces to encourage the production of new sprays which are so attractive when picked in bud and watched as they open in the house. Sometimes one sees arches of jasmine trained over doorways which have become a congested mass of woody stems with only shortened sprigs of blossom, all grace and beauty clipped away. Shaded or semi-shaded walls produce the longest shoots. Any type of soil will do, but it is always wise to dig a large hole and add whatever vegetable waste you can find to improve it. The soil under walls is often very compacted and dry, if not full of builder's rubbish.

The summer flowering jasmine is called *Jasminum officinale*. It is very vigorous with attractive pinnate leaves and clusters of sweetly scented white flowers, most noticeable on warm evenings. There are two variegated forms of this species. One has large leaves rather coarsely splashed with yellow. In some settings this brassy piebald effect might be advantageous, but I prefer the silver variegated form. This plant is less vigorous initially, although in time it will reach the roof of a large house. In full summer leaf it is a beautiful sight as long tendrils cascade from a wall, or maybe wind themselves round the balustrade of a stone staircase a-flutter with finely cut leaves delicately patterned in cream, pink and green. There is also a yellow variegated form of winter jasmine.

Jasminum nudiflorum

Tellima grandiflora 'Rubra'

Tellima grandiflora 'Rubra'

This rather pompous title belongs to a modest plant which, like modest people, gains your affection on closer acquaintance. It is at its best when times are bad. Throughout January I admire the tidy colourful clumps in the garden and now I have picked a leaf coated with hoar frost which is melting, like sugar icing, into a little pool of water on my table. Quite undamaged, the leaf is shaped not unlike an ivy leaf, but with round scalloped edges. The texture is slightly rough because of a covering of minute bristly hairs. But it is the colour which draws you. The surface of each leaf is dark mahogany-red, with a matt-silk texture. As contrast the back of each leaf is carmine-rose, the glistening surface broken by the raised pattern of veins. Arranged in low-growing clusters both sides of the leaves catch the winter sunlight where they decorate the edge of a border.

When spring comes these leaves will dwindle as new fresh green ones push their way through them. By May, many slender stems, about 18 inches high, will carry spires of small, pale green bells with frilly edges which turn pink as they age. They are not in the least 'Grandiflora', but are delicate to look at in the garden and pretty to pick. The leaves will stay green until the autumn frosts when the rich winter colour will return.

Tellima grandiflora itself has much less richly coloured leaves. I think seedlings vary slightly; one I have has dark veins, but does not assume the warm red tints in winter.

Tellima grandiflora is an American plant related to *Heuchera*. One of its relatives, *Heuchera americana* (*H. richardsonii*, *H. rubescens*), also called Satin Leaf, is also much valued for the beauty of its leaves. In this case it is the new young leaves which are an exquisite blend of soft orange-tan and brown shades, maturing to green with copper-brown shading while the main veins are faintly picked out in palest green. The wide spires of tiny green and brown flowers are of secondary interest, but they intrigue flower arrangers. New leaves continue to be produced until autumn, staying in good condition until spring.

Both *Tellima grandiflora* and *Heuchera americana* will thrive in sun or part shade in retentive soil. They are easily grown under north walls in town gardens, or among trees and shrubs where it does not become desperately dry. They appreciate a dressing of leaf mould or vegetable compost.

The good forms are best propagated by division.

Green Hellebores

In January the green of winter hellebores stands out like a light among fallen leaves and bare twigs. There are in fact several, but I am thinking of two most generally grown. The first, *Helleborus foetidus*, the smaller of the two, is a native. Each plant has several thick stems closely set with holly-green, fan-shaped leaves which are narrowly divided, creating a dark, interlaced effect. Rising above them a stout flower stem is immediately eye-catching, enclosed in large, palest green bracts. Slowly it unfolds itself into a much branched head of drooping bell-like flowers, looking not unlike a bunch of pale green grapes. By March these will have opened more widely, with some forms showing a narrow magenta-red rim around the edge of each bell. These plants are about 18 inches high and across.

Helleborus corsicus (*H. argutifolius, H. lividus corsicus*) makes a larger, almost shrub-like plant with twenty or thirty stems on well grown plants. Their leaves are larger and paler, netted with veins, divided into three claw-shaped segments, making a handsome dome of foliage over 2 ft. high, more than 4 ft. across. The flowers too are larger, cup-shaped like small, pale green water-lilies, arranged in a huge upturned bouquet, which open their first flowers in December, illuminating the garden until May. With both these hellebores it is the sharp contrast in tones of green which makes them so dramatically beautiful.

Helleborus viridis makes large deeply cut leaves in summer which die away completely in winter. The flowers in spring are usually a brilliant pure green, but there are slight variations. I have seen one in which it was a pleasure to look into the hearts of the flowers and see the blue shade inside caused by a faint waxy bloom. *H. v. occidentalis* is a native of Britain. It is smaller flowered and larger leafed, but no less attractive.

Other excellent and easily grown hellebores are to be found under the title *H. orientalis*. These include plants with seductive flowers in fruity shades of plum and purple, but I have one that is considered to be a good form of *H. kochii*, which some botanists believe to be the true *H. orientalis*. My plants form crowded clumps of short branching stems covered in January with round yellowish-green buds which open nicely rounded, almost primrose coloured nodding flowers.

All hellebores like soil rich with leaf mould, preferably in part shade, but they will do well in sun provided the soil is enriched with humus. They can be grown from seed which germinates easily if sown when ripe, sometimes in June or July.

Helleborus foetidus

Cyclamen hederifolium

Hardy Cyclamens

There are many different kinds of wild cyclamens. Those found in sun-drenched countries like Greece or Crete are rather tender, and generally need to be grown in an alpine house or frame. My favourites are those which survive outside despite weeks of worryingly low temperatures. When frost and snow have melted, it is heart-warming to find such comfortable clusters of leaves, so fresh and fair — there really is not another plant to excel them in the winter garden.

I have planted mine around the base of an old oak tree. To retain moisture and prevent mass germination of weed seedlings I have covered the bed with a layer, 1–2 inches deep, of pulverized bark. Peat or clean leaf mould would do.

One of the hardiest and best is *Cyclamen neapolitanum*, now correctly known as *C. hederifolium*. This is a good name because the leaves do remind one of ivy leaves, but they are greatly enhanced by the marbled effect of silvery-green designs 'painted' over a dark green background. Scarcely two plants are identical. The flowers, freely produced in shades of pink and including a very fine white, are one of the loveliest sights in autumn.

An endearing little cyclamen which flowers throughout the winter is to be found under a confusion of names. *C. coum* (of gardens) has plain green leaves with glossy purple backs. They are almost round in shape, about the size of a ten-penny piece.

Cyclamen orbiculatum (which means round and flat) and its varieties (including *C. atkinsii*) are very similar, but the leaves are marbled with silvery-green patterns. Both these cyclamens flower in December and January if the weather is mild, continuing to delight well into spring. Such a joy it is to find these short-petalled, chubby little flowers lighting up the leaf-litter around the base of old trees. They come in all shades from bright crimson-purple to pink and white, each with a conspicuous dark patch at the base of the petals.

Cyclamens can be grown from seed which looks like snails' eggs, palest pink in colour, falling in late August from fat round seed pods spiralled close against the bosom of the parent plant. Sow them immediately as they are difficult to germinate if allowed to dry out. Sometimes you can part the leaves of old plants to find plenty of tiny newly germinated babies which can be gently lifted off the leaf mould accumulated on top of the old corm, and potted until they are large enough to fend for themselves.

Hamamelis mollis

The Chinese Witch Hazel, *Hamamelis mollis*, is a shrub of surprises. It looks unlike anything else except members of its own tribe, and I never can say for sure when it will be in flower. In a mild winter it will be opening buds on New Year's Day, in colder winters it will be February or later. The sight and scent of a shrub in full flower when the temperature is right is always breathtaking.

It makes a rather gawky shrub, stiffly spreading, with flowers scattered like tassels all over the bare twigs. Brown velvety buds open, each with four narrow strap-shaped petals, bright yellow and curled like those party whistles which you blow down to make them unroll. They are held in maroon-red calyces, and occur on short spurs, several clustered together to make greater effect. Only very severe frost seems to damage the petals. If it is too cold to smell them outside, the warmth of a room will draw out the perfume, sweet and fresh, like primroses.

These spidery flowers need a good background, preferably something evergreen, facing the sun to warm their petals. In summer the shrub is good looking with large, soft, hazel-shaped leaves which turn yellow in autumn.

While *Hamamelis mollis* is the shrub most commonly seen there are other named forms. Although none, in my opinion, are superior to *H. mollis* some are interesting and worth growing if you have space to experiment. *H. mollis* 'Pallida' is very attractive with much paler lemon-yellow flowers borne in densely crowded clusters along winter-bare branches. Other hybrids tend to have yellow flowers suffused with red which gives them an orange appearance from a distance. They are not my favourites, but many hybrids have been raised, and it is best to see well-grown specimens before passing judgement on all of them.

Hamamelis virginiana from E. America is the commercial source of the astringent 'witch hazel'. It produces not very conspicuous small yellow flowers in autumn, often before the leaves fall so one scarcely notices them; but the autumn colour, a fine golden yellow, is attractive.

Hamamelises like well-drained soil but not too dry; leaf mould or well-wetted peat helps when planting. The price asked for this treasure reflects neither the value nor the art required to propagate it. You will also be asked for time and patience to grow it into a fine shrub. The dormant season is the best time to plant.

Hamamelis mollis

Prunus subhirtella 'Autumnalis Rosea'

Prunus subhirtella

This name covers a varied group of small flowering cherries whose season extends from autumn till spring. Probably the best known is *Prunus subhirtella* 'Autumnalis'. The most memorable I have seen was planted outside a wide window overlooking a little paved garden. Drawn into the bay of the window was the dining table, and there we sat, one winter's day, many years ago, in a world of tiny snowflake blossoms, with blue tits fluttering among them. My friend has gone, and maybe the tree too, but the picture remains in my mind.

I have planted the pink form, *P. s.* 'Autumnalis Rosea', with deep rose-pink buds which open semi-double shell-pink flowers. The tree is light and dainty in habit, with twiggy branches closely set with buds which usually open a few blossoms in autumn and continue to open others sparingly throughout any mild spell in winter, generally reserving the main show for March. But much depends on the weather and the bullfinches. The males, handsome as small parrots with glossy blue-black heads, red-flushed breasts and large, well-designed bills, would sit with their wives on my tree and strip it of every last bud if I did nothing to check them. I have tried spraying with bitter-tasting deterrents, but still I lost my blossoms. Now we save our milk bottle tops and make a necklace which rattles in the wind. Bullfinches are timid birds (notice that winter cherries in roadside gardens never lose their blossoms, nor Forsythia, which also gets stripped in my quiet country garden).

Another early flowering tree which I feel ashamed not to possess, since it has twice been extolled in letters to me by Graham S. Thomas, is *Prunus mume*. I have looked it up in Hillier's *Manual of Trees and Shrubs*, where I see that it is also called 'Japanese Apricot'. It forms a small tree with green young shoots, and the type has single, almond scented, pink flowers which pale as they age. In very mild winters it may be in flower in January, but the normal time is March. This tree is extensively cultivated in Japan, so, not surprisingly, there are several named forms, including white, pink, and double flowers.

Both these trees benefit from a position sheltered from icy north-east winds which damage the early flowers. They need a deep retentive soil well enriched with compost. Planting can be done at any time during the dormant season.

Coronilla glauca

Although not entirely hardy, this small shrub is a delight in mid-winter, a picture of unforced gaiety, responding to every mild spell. A few degrees of frost do not harm the opened blossoms and only prolonged cold, with temperatures well below freezing, will seriously affect the bush. My garden is in the southern half of the country, but is probably as cold as most when arctic weather comes hurling out of the north east. Situated under a south wall in well-drained, gravelly soil, my *Coronilla* is covered each winter with clusters of small, bright yellow pea flowers, and will remain so well into the summer. There is scarcely a month when a blossom cannot be found; the shape and habit is neat and graceful; smooth green stems divide and redivide, while every new shoot is tipped with tightly rolled bundles of buds. The leaves are attractive all the year round; they are small, wedge shaped, and of a bluish-green colour.

There is a form in which the leaves are broadly edged with creamy-white, *Coronilla glauca* 'Variegata'. The effect is very light and pale, with fewer but taller branches which create a delicate pattern against the wall. Both are good to pick, and would make good tub plants in a cool conservatory.

Not suitable for heavy cold soils, coronillas grow tough on poor rations in light soil. They need to be established during spring and early summer with possibly a little protection the first winter. Occasionally I have lost an old bush during a prolonged cold spell and the following season quite a crop of seedlings have appeared which I had not noticed before. Cuttings are easily rooted, so if you find no seedlings a few young shoots stuck around the edge of a pot in late summer and stood on the window-sill for the winter will be an insurance, and if not needed can be given away.

I have *Coronilla valentina* humped over the corner of a low raised bed, sheltered by walls of the house. It makes a gnarled-looking trunk, being slow growing and rather congested in habit. It has survived several hard winters and cheers me in the dark months, even when snow-covered, with the odd cluster of sweetly scented flowers. When winter's back is turned all caution is abandoned as it flaunts for weeks a dazzling dress of glowing yellow.

Coronilla glauca

Sasa veitchii

Sasa veitchii

During the winter months many visitors to my garden pause by this curiously handsome plant, although few should allow it through their own front gate. It used to be called *Arundinaria veitchii*, so you will guess that it is a kind of bamboo. It grows not much above 3 ft. high which is good because you can look down on to it. The bad thing is its dreadfully invasive habit. Strong, thick shoots push underground to re-emerge and grow through everything around. But if you happen to have a bit of derelict woodland, an isolated patch of clay, or farm reservoir banks which could be planted with coarse-growing plants to make an interesting feature instead of an eyesore, then this bamboo is one of the most effective things you could choose.

My colonies are planted on the clay banks of the reservoir which separates my garden from the neighbouring farm. They have done an excellent job binding the steep slippery sides, providing impenetrable thickets of low, dense ground-cover between groups of coloured stemmed willows and dogwoods. They produce new stems each spring and summer set with bright green leaves, remarkable for their size, more than 6 inches long, and as much as 2 inches across. When autumn comes the colour is withdrawn from the edges of the leaves so they are left with broad cream margins which gives the appearance of bold and attractive variegation. Undamaged by bad weather this unusual bamboo makes a focal point valued in the winter landscape by the designer and photographer. It is not easily found but some enterprising nurseries do have it for those who have space to accommodate it.

A genuinely variegated bamboo, and more easily obtainable, is *Arundinaria viridistriata* (*A. auricoma*), the Golden-leafed Bamboo. It is among the loveliest, safe in any garden as it spreads very slowly. It can help to create a very natural leafy effect especially if planted with other bamboos in a town garden, and may be planted in suitable containers if watering is not neglected. The ribbon-like leaflets are a soft, warm shade of yellow, varyingly striped and shaded with light green, as though they were hand painted.

I cut the old canes down in late winter so that invigorated young shoots spring up with bright new foliage, unspoilt by tattered remains. One season's growth is just over 3 ft. high. In very sheltered gardens they could be left to create a much taller feature.

Bamboos are propagated by division in spring. The freshly divided pieces need to be protected from drying winds until they are established.

Snowdrops

This is the best time of year to think of planting snowdrops. Wait until the flowers are beginning to fade, then dig up the bulbs 'in green', that is, in full leaf. Separate them gently, and replant them immediately, in drifts singly, or in scattered clumps. If you cannot beg a spadeful of bulbs from a friend, or barter with a stranger for something nice in return, then you can buy them from a bulb merchant's catalogue, and plant them dry in autumn, but they will take longer to establish.

They do not like to be baked in summer, so the shade of trees or leaf-losing shrubs suits them well. They will grow in most soils provided there is adequate humus, but they do best on heavier soils, especially chalky soils in semi-shade.

Children love snowdrops, marvelling over the first one, or losing themselves in a copse carpeted with thousands of icy white drooping heads. It is later in life that we learn with surprise how many variations there are.

The earliest to flower is *Galanthus nivalis reginae-olgae*, which suddenly appears in late autumn without leaves. They follow during the winter. *Galanthus nivalis* is the common snowdrop. The old-fashioned double form makes a long-lasting display, and increases well while a curious form called *G. n.* 'Viridapicis' has green tips to the normally pure white outer petals. It is worth trying to obtain *G. caucasicus* which has large bold flowers above handsome grey foliage, but it increases best if moved 'in green'.

As they have been loved and grown for centuries there are now many hybrid forms of snowdrop. Some are named with certainty, others are not. Some are so similar you need good eyesight to see the difference. But others are so distinct they ensnare you to seek more, to peer into the face of every fresh encounter to see if it is a treasure. Among the doubles there are several which have tightly packed, perfectly even central segments looking like green and white Victorian posies.

I have a late flowering snowdrop which is still fresh and impressive in mid-March when all others have faded. It has large globular flowers and is probably a form of *G. byzantinus*. Held in my hand in a warm room I notice its strange musky perfume which several snowdrops have.

Galanthus nivalis

Hedera helix poetica 'Arborea'

Hedera helix poetica 'Arborea'

This rarely seen form of ivy deserves to be more widely known. There are all too few hardy, handsome, and reasonably small evergreen shrubs which make good background furnishing, especially in winter.

I obtained my first plant from a cutting I found in an old neglected garden over 30 years ago. It never trails but forms a dense slow-growing bush. It was originally produced by rooting the matured fruiting stems of a form of *Hedera helix* found wild in Greece and Turkey. In January, my present bush — now over 20 years old, about 5 ft. high and as much across — is covered with drooping clusters of bright green fruits. Throughout the spring these berries will slowly turn to soft orange-yellow, very effective massed against the bright green, glossy narrow leaves. (Our own native Common Ivy produces black fruits.)

An arrangement of trailing stems taken from other forms of *H. helix*, with perhaps a few sprays of the softly variegated *H. h.* 'Lutzii' which has small leaves prettily mottled in shades of green and primrose, would be well set off by several fine heads of these unusual berries.

My bush is sheltered in a rather shady situation, but in an open position the old leaves are said to turn bright copper colour in winter, with veins remaining green. I must hurry to start another plant soon, in an exposed site.

It is fortunate there are so many climbing forms of ivy available since they provide us with one of the most attractive and useful of winter evergreens. Not only can they be used to cover unsightly walls or tree stumps; they can also be used very effectively as ground-cover under wide spreading trees where scarcely grass will grow. The large-leafed forms are especially good for this.

One of my favourites is *Hedera colchica* 'Sulphur Heart', much better known as 'Paddy's Pride'. Each leaf looks as though it were painted in shades of green, the colour deepest at the edges, but smudging irregularly towards the pale centre which is intensified with a network of yellow veins.

Ivies take time to become established, but once they have put down strong roots they grow vigorously. Old specimens need to be pruned every few years to encourage long trails of fine leaves.

Narcissus minor 'Cedric Morris'

This little wild daffodil was found by chance, near a roadside in northern Spain, about 30 years ago, by the artist and gardener the late Sir Cedric Morris. The most remarkable thing about it is its time of flowering. If the winter is average, that is if we have no really severe weather in December, then it will invariably produce buds and the odd open flower for Christmas Day. Throughout January and February its flowers remain fresh, new buds open and the stems elongate, up to 10 inches. Each little flower is a perfectly shaped trumpet daffodil, about one inch long and across; not at all insignificant. The base of the petals is shaded green, and the whole flower, including the frilled and fluted trumpet, is light lemon-yellow. During very severe weather the flower stems will collapse and lie stuck to the ground with frost, but when the thaw comes they will stand up again, fresh and undamaged.

Once established into clumps of flowering bulbs it makes a pretty sight in the garden in February, and is most cheering if brought into the house with a handful of snowdrops.

With such a rarity it is well to be warned of the evil narcissus fly, whose eggs develop into fat white grubs which eat out the heart of a bulb. I have learnt that this fly dislikes shade, so I plant my dwarf narcissi around the base of small deciduous shrubs, or where the foliage of larger plants will overshadow them.

Building up stocks of narcissi by natural increase takes many years so it is worth knowing another way to increase them. Take a strong clean bulb and remove loose brown scales. Using a sharp clean knife cut it into segments, like slices of cake, from neck to base. Small bulbs of dwarf narcissi could be divided into 8 pieces, each piece having a portion of basal plate with scales attached. Dip the pieces into a fungicidal solution for 30 minutes (Benlate or Captafol). Drain them, and place in a pierced polythene bag, well mixed up with dampened vermiculite, or a peat/sand mix. Leave in a warm sheltered place, keep damp but not wet. After a few weeks tiny bulbils will be seen at the base of each piece. These can be individually potted (or set into pans) and grown on until large enough to plant outside. They will take 3–4 years to reach flowering size.

Narcissi need enriched soil to make good bulbs. Poor sands and gravels, or waterlogged soils are not suitable.

Narcissus minor 'Cedric Morris'

Iris unguicularis

Iris unguicularis

This Iris, found wild in sandy soil in Algeria, used to be called *Iris stylosa* and would be on my list of ten top garden plants. When the weather is at its worst, and life's problems appear more insoluble than usual, it is a blessing to go into the garden and search for the slim buds tucked among narrow, strap-shaped evergreen leaves. When taken into the house the warmth of the room soon causes them to open, and you are aware of the sweet fresh perfume, reminiscent of primroses.

I always marvel, at this bleak time of year, at the size of these exquisite flowers, and the delicate texture of their broad flaring petals finely pencilled and shaded with darker veins. Planted at the foot of a warm south-facing wall in gritty, well-drained soil an established clump will often produce a flower or two for Christmas, but by February it will be full of flowers, with buds to follow. Several selected and named forms can be found. My favourite is 'Walter Butt' which has the largest flowers, of very pale lavender-blue, produced most generously. The commonly known form has light purplish-blue flowers, while those of 'Mary Barnard' are deep violet blue. There is also a rare white form, with unfortunately a delicate constitution, and smaller flowers. It helps the display if you remove some of the tangle of old leaves and also look out for snails and cutworms which sometimes attack the buds before they open. Transplanting freshly lifted plants is best done in September, when new roots are being made.

The distribution of *Iris unguicularis* extends from Algeria to the other end of the Mediterranean and beyond. From districts near the Black Sea comes *I. u. lazica*, not so remarkable as the forms I have already mentioned but interesting. It has smaller flowers with narrower petals which are dark violet-blue produced among a wealth of broad, rich green leaves. The forms found in Crete have the narrowest leaves with good flowers in miniature, but they seem to need very warm conditions to flower regularly and well. Both these latter forms are scentless.

Pussy Willows

Most of us know the handsome yellow catkins of Pussy Willow or Palm which is *Salix caprea*, our native Goat Willow. It is often seen growing along the roadside on the damp edge of a field ditch. There are many other willows which have been introduced to gardens which are very ornamental. They differ considerably in size of bush and style of catkin.

Salix melanostachys will come more easily to mind if you remember that melancholy means a dark mood. This sturdy bush is remarkable for its black catkins which open to show a glint of ruby red before exploding into a mass of yellow pollen. In total contrast is *S. daphnoides*, the Violet Willow, which makes a small tree. Here a dark purple framework is overlaid with white bloom, while from it cascade long slender shoots set with the silkiest of catkins, looking in my garden like large raindrops falling into the pool of dark water behind them.

For smaller gardens *S. hastata* 'Wehrhahnii' is ideal. It will thrive in any good retentive soil and grows slowly to about the size of a large blackcurrant bush. The young shoots are smooth and very dark chocolate brown, and so are the closely set fat buds which burst to show the neatest and whitest of all 'pussy willow' catkins, like small buds of cotton wool.

Equally attractive, but opposite in form is *S. repens argentea*. This semi-prostrate willow looks best if pruned almost to the ground each year after flowering. Then it will produce many graceful slender stems, up to 3 ft. long, set in summer with small, silvery, silky leaves. In spring the pearl-like catkins, exploding to yellow are a joy, especially when placed to arch over a small pool.

For those gardeners who have heavy retentive soil and plenty of space *S. sachalinensis* 'Sekka' makes a fast growing, wide spreading shrub. In March it is a glorious sight when its long wands are wreathed in yellow, pollen-loaded catkins. Occasional branches, not all, look as though several had been stuck together and then flattened, and they continue to grow in weirdly attractive curves, forming a ready-made 'Japanese' arrangement. If you cut these branches when the catkins are small and silvery-pink, stand them in a mixture of glycerine and hot water for a few days and then hang them up to dry, they will remain in perfect condition for years until you grow tired of them.

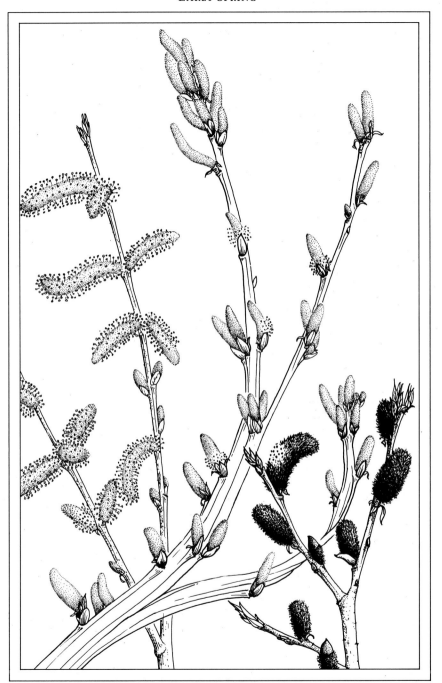

Salix species

Cornus mas

Cornus mas

I shall never forget my first sight of this unusual small tree. Cycling one winter's day past an abandoned old shrubbery I caught a glimpse of something yellow struggling to reach the light from among choking hollies and laurel. I managed to reach a slender leafless twig and was mystified by the closely held clusters of little starry yellow flowers which I did not recognize. Although not nearly so showy as the brassy forsythias (which in my garden are stripped in bud by bullfinches) these dainty sprays created a most charming effect against the dark wintry background.

Now, many years later, I have in my own garden a large shrub or small dense tree which has grown slowly to about 12 ft. high and 10 ft. wide. Still, to my surprise and chagrin, it has never produced for me the round, red, edible fruits it should, but in late autumn the pointed oval leaves sometimes produce good colour. It has also just occurred to me that its strong frame would provide a good support for a late flowering clematis, perhaps the pink clematis 'Comtesse de Bouchard', with a planting of hardy fuchsias at the base, while in spring the vivid *Scilla sibirica* already creates a blue carpet beneath the haze of greenish-yellow blossom.

Almost any soil, short of poor starved gravel, suits *Cornus mas*, and any situation except dense shade. *C. mas*, though seldom seen, has long been cultivated, so there are several forms available. 'Aurea' has leaves suffused with yellow. 'Elegantissima' has leaves variegated yellow and flushed pink, best shaded from strong sunlight. 'Macrocarpa' produces larger fruits than the type. I wonder if it sets fruit more generously too. I have recently acquired *C. m.* 'Variegata' whose smaller leaves are irregularly margined with cream. This is one of the most beautiful variegated shrubs we can grow, ideal for a choice position in small gardens. It is best suited in a cool, partly shaded situation.

Cornus mas, the cornelian cherry, is at its best when the Chinese Witch Hazel, *Hamamelis mollis* is beginning to fade. It looks so fresh and spring-like when picked and arranged in a long low container, perhaps in the Japanese style, to form a flowering tree beneath which you can group snowdrops, or palest blue scillas among a few sprays of small-leafed ivy.

Winter Heathers

Each winter I value most those plants which retain fresh and healthy foliage. I like to see the bare structural bones of the garden when abundant summer growth has vanished, but those trees, shrubs or plants which retain good foliage, however severe the weather, save the garden from drab formlessness.

Among the brightest of my winter jewels are several heathers, not because they are in flower, but because of their shape and vivid, coloured leaves. Planted together I have several which glow defiantly when the garden is chilled with freezing fog, but whose brilliant orange, red and copper tones are kindled into a blaze on a day of rare winter sunshine.

Calluna vulgaris, the Common Ling, makes a rather spikily shaped bush. There are several named varieties including 'Gold Feather', 'Gold Haze' and 'Blazeaway'. In summer all have attractive yellowish-green foliage which stands well among dark green varieties. Another heather in my colourful group is a form of *Erica cinerea*, the Bell Heather called 'Golden Drop', which is smothered with bright rose bells in late summer. But in winter its low mould of soft strokable foliage is one of the most brilliant, enamelled in shades of coral-red. With both these heathers the winter colour is best where fully exposed. If you pick one of the long coppery-red spikes of *Calluna* you will notice it is pale green on the shadier side.

Both require a lime-free soil with peat well incorporated, and ideally a peat mulch to conserve moisture. If your soil contains lime there are other heathers, including *E. carnea* and its varieties, which provide winter flowers.

Another fine winter flowering heather which makes a really substantial shrub is *E. × darleyensis*. It forms a large hummock, as much as 4 ft. across and tall, providing sprays of lilac-pink blossom to cheer the house through-out the winter months. It is still bright and fresh in March when it is most heartening to see a few foraging honey bees, busily breaking their long winter hibernation with this rich source of pollen and nectar. 'Arthur Johnson' is a good selected form of this heather with deeper lilac-pink flowers on longer, more elegant spikes. Careful pruning every two or three years will encourage the production of these fine spikes of blossom.

Erica cinerea 'Golden Drop'

Primula denticulata

The Drumstick Primula

Primula denticulata, the Drumstick Primula, forms a tight round ball of buds which emerges at soil level in early March when late snowdrops are still in flower, opening its first flower or two at ground level, impatient to see what is going on. Over a period of several weeks the stem lengthens to about 10 inches, and the buds open to form a dense globe of tightly packed, small, primrose-like flowers poised on top of the stem. It is fortunate that late spring frosts do not damage the opening flowers. The emerging leaves, stems, and buds are lightly dusted with a golden-green powder, called farina.

The original type, found in open birch woods and meadows in the Himalayas, was clear pale lavender, cool contrast to the rosettes of light green leaves, but variations have been selected and now there are good white forms, and coloured forms including rich carmine and purple, all with small yellow eyes. However, not all seedlings raised are good. In some, the individual flowers are small or washy coloured. It is best, if you can obtain it, to sow primula seed as soon as it is ripe, when it will germinate easily.

If you have an established clump, particularly if it is an extra fine form, you can divide it to make more. You can also take root cuttings. Dig up a strong plant while still in flower. Remove about half of the long white string-like roots. Remove the flowers, reduce the leaf, and separate the plant into individual rosettes. Replant them in a sheltered place, or pot them until they are recovered before planting out again. Meanwhile cut the roots into pieces, about $1\frac{1}{2} - 2$ inches long, keeping them top side up on your potting table. Prepare a pan, and insert the cuttings around the edge, or across in rows if you have enough. Just cover the tops with sand or sifted soil. Water well and stand in a cool sheltered place. In two months or so you will see little shoots begin to appear. When they are large enough gently remove them from the pan, pot individually, and grow on under shelter until they are sufficiently established to be planted out in their final positions.

These plants prefer a heavy soil which does not dry out, in sun, or part shade, and can be planted in autumn or spring. They make handsome leafy clumps for the rest of the growing season. They look best grouped along the edge of a partially shaded border, perhaps beneath apple trees, or in a cool, north-facing pocket in the rock garden.

Ribes laurifolium

Most people know the red-flowering currant, *Ribes sanguineum*, which flowers on long, almost leafless stems in April. Not so well known is the green-flowered *R. laurifolium* which opens its first flowers in February and is in full bloom by mid March. It makes a low sprawly bush suitable for a rock garden where it would look splendid draped over a large rock. In my garden it sprawls over a low bank, and also fits a curve on the front edge of a shrubbery where I suddenly come across its pale blossoms, unexpected so early in the year. The almost horizontal branches are set with large, narrowly oval leaves which when young have red flushed backs and stalks. In late February, from the tip of every shoot, pale green buds appear, and from them unroll short racemes of tiny, pale green flowers. Each flower has a dark green enamelled eye which gleams as though it were a minute pool of nectar, no doubt to entice some trusting insect. At the base of each individual flower stem is a long, narrow, transparent green bract, almost as long as the flower, which emphasizes the pale whitish-green look of the whole inflorescence. I can imagine flower arrangers removing the leaves which do partially hide the flowers and can look a little tatty by the end of winter, but in the garden the contrast of strong dark foliage and delicate clusters of flower is quietly attractive. Unfortunately there is no perfume. If it were scented like the daphnes this little shrub would probably be much better known.

I have read that this shrub forms berries which turn from red to black. Feeling very unobservant since I have never seen a sign of fruit I looked into the matter and discovered that there are male and female bushes.

There are several other decorative forms of *Ribes*. *R. speciosum* might be called the Fuchsia-flowered Gooseberry. It makes a semi-evergreen shrub which, if regularly pruned, produces wand-like branches covered with reddish-brown bristles. These are hung along their entire length with slender fuchsia-like flowers, garnet-red and most beautiful when seen with evening light shining through them. This shrub needs a warm site to look its best.

Ribes sanguineum 'Brocklebankii' is the lovely yellow-leafed form of flowering currant, but it needs protection from strong sunlight which will scorch its delicate foliage.

All these shrubs need retentive soil and can be propagated from cuttings.

Ribes laurifolium

Helleborus orientalis

The Lenten Roses

These lovely plants are commonly grouped under the name *Helleborus orientalis*. Easier to grow than the Christmas Rose (*H. niger*) they provide us with some of the most sumptuous of all garden flowers. Because it is an interbred group, plants grown from seed provide all the thrill of a lucky dip.

The colours are exquisite and individual flowers may be greenish cream, green and white, pink and green, burgundy red or shades of purple. The flower stems stand 15–18 inches tall, with many stems to an established clump, each carrying several flowers. Some will droop like globular lamp-shades, hiding heavily speckled or spotted hearts. The best of these may be creamy white or deep rose pink, and found under the name *H. guttatus*, which means spotted. Others may open wider to show cream-coloured stamens set in olive-green nectaries, contrasted against dark plum-purple petals. They flower from February to April, and are followed by large handsome evergreen leaves which act both as a feature and ground-cover for the rest of the year.

Helleborus atrorubens is similar to some of the *H. orientalis* hybrids of which it is a parent, but it loses its leaves in winter. Its flowers appear early in January, together with the Christmas Rose, *H. niger*, and last well into March. They are soft plum-purple, nodding on short branched stems about 12 inches tall.

Another early flowering form I have is *H. kochii* which some botanists consider to be the true *H. orientalis*. Each plant throws up scores of branching stems scarcely more than 15 inches tall, bowed with hundreds of drooping buds and flowers which open pale primrose-yellow faintly shadowed with green.

Deep rich soil suits these plants best, in part shade. Dig a large hole, in a north or east facing border, fill it with well-rotted compost, mix it thoroughly, then put in your plant. A mulch will keep the roots cool in summer.

Extra fine forms can only be increased by division. I find the best time to do this is March. I snip off the flowers, cut the plants into rooted pieces, each bearing a new leaf shoot. Provided they are not shriven by cold east winds the pieces take well. Large clumps lifted and moved intact never seem to recover their old vigour.

Seed should be sown when ripe in mid-summer, or by the autumn when it will germinate freely in spring. Seed sown in spring usually waits a year before germinating. When the heavy seed pods look almost ready, early in June, we shroud them with old tights to catch the shiny black seeds before the capsules explode.

Brunnera macrophylla

Brunnera macrophylla, which used to be called *Anchusa myosotidiflora* (Myosotis is the Latin name for Forget-me-not), is a joy for weeks on end in spring, with its delicate bouquets of tiny, vivid, Forget-me-not-like flowers. In mild winters the flower stems are already emerging through the leaf-litter, sometimes opening very cautiously, one or two specks of blossom from among the heads of tightly packed buds. As the weeks go by flower stems elongate and branch until a soft haze of blue is formed, about 18 inches high. As the flowers finally fade in May new basal leaves, heart-shaped, large as tea plates, matt textured and dark green are ready to replace prettiness with bold dramatic design. Some people find the contrast between dainty flowers and engulfing foliage too great, but in the right setting the large simple leaves make much needed contrast among small or delicate leafed plants. I like to see them among running carpets of *Viola cornuta* or *Tiarella cordifolia*, with perhaps a touch of gold, in the shape of Bowles' Golden Grass, *Milium effusum* 'Aureum', to lighten the scene.

Brunnera macrophylla grows wild in the deciduous forests of the Caucasian mountains, facing the Black Sea. In gardens it will grow in almost any soil, preferably in soil which does not dry out, in shade or part shade.

There are other good garden forms. *B. m.* 'Variegata' is one of the most dramatic of all variegated plants. The central zone of each heart-shaped leaf is marbled greyish-green and surrounded by a broad, ivory-white border. Some leaves are almost entirely white. But this plant is not easy to grow. It needs a cool site sheltered from strong sunlight and must never be deprived of moisture because the white variegation is very delicate and browns easily.

Brunnera macrophylla 'Hadspen Cream', introduced by Eric Smith, is less dramatic but it is, I think, preferable. Its leaves are a softer combination of light green and deep cream or primrose. I find this plant easier to place and grow, but it still needs part shade and good retentive soil.

Finally, *B. m.* 'Langtrees', which originated in the garden of Dr. Tony Rogerson in Devon, has dark green leaves evenly marked with a border of large silvery-white spots which look as if they had been applied with a brushful of metallic paint.

In propagating these selected forms be careful to keep only the crowns with variegated leaves. Plants grown from root cuttings will have plain green leaves.

Brunnera macrophylla 'Variegata'

Pulmonaria saccharata

Pulmonaria, or Lungwort

The name *Pulmonaria* (Lungwort) refers to the spots and blotches which cover the leaves of some of these plants. They reminded the old botanists of diseased lungs. It is not an attractive simile but there are happier nicknames, including 'Soldiers and Sailors', suggested by the red and blue flowers which appear at the same time. *Pulmonaria* is practically the first herbaceous plant to flower after the long winter, and the different forms and variations keep up a display for weeks, indeed for months.

Pulmonaria officinalis is the best-known form, making neat clumps of small, heart-shaped, rather bristly leaves which are covered with silvery white spots. Pink buds open soft red tubular flowers which quickly change to blue.

The earliest in my garden is *P. angustifolia* 'Munstead Blue'. The low clumps of velvety green leaves are unspotted, and the pink buds immediately open rich gentian-blue flowers on short stems, creating a pool of blue beneath leafless shrubs.

Pulmonaria rubra has coral-red flowers without a touch of blue, followed by large, matt, apple-green leaves, also without spots.

The largest flowers and spots are produced by *P. saccharata*. Much larger flower heads open deep rose-pink flowers which fade to mauvish-purple. When they look untidy they should be cut off to make way for the splendid basal leaves spread out as great rosettes, dark bristly green, evenly mottled with large silvery-green spots, making a fine feature in a shady border for the rest of the season.

While loved for their early flowers pulmonarias are valued perhaps more as ground-cover, beneath trees or among shrubs. The plants can easily be divided and planted to form large, weed-smothering clumps. They cross-fertilize freely so good selected forms are best increased by division.

Pulmonaria saccharata 'Argentea' produces rosettes of leaves almost entirely silvered which look like huge pale flowers lying against the dark leaf mould, wonderful contrast with purple-leafed *Viola labradorica*.

Pulmonaria longifolia, makes flattish rosettes of long, narrow, pointed leaves which are dark green, heavily spotted with silvery-white. During spring and early summer it produces quaint round heads of small, deep blue flowers held well above the leaves.

Pulmonarias will grow in any fertile soil in shade or part-shade. They do best in humus-rich retentive soil. There is a tendency to mildew if they suffer too dry conditions.

Valeriana phu 'Aurea'

While most of the daffodil buds show scarcely a slit of yellow (a tantalizing hint of golden glory to come), my plants of *Valeriana phu* 'Aurea' are already bringing colour to the garden, and will not be outshone when April sunshine has unfolded sheets of daffodils. This may sound an exaggeration when you realize that I am talking about the leaves of a plant, but I assure you that it is not. This plant is grown for its clusters of young divided leaves which are a wonderful clear yellow. They make an unusually vivid accent in early spring, surrounded by the coppery tints of new unfolding buds on shrubs, or the coloured stems of dogwoods and willows.

In a group which pleases me I have a very dark plum-coloured form of *Helleborus orientalis* which alone could look a little sombre, but its beautiful dusky heads appear to be lit by the light reflected from the yellow-leafed *Valeriana* planted nearby. Adding sharp touches of scarlet-red are young shoots of *Euphorbia sikkimensis* which runs among them. By the middle of May the leaves will have matured green, and you cease to notice the plants until suddenly, in August, you are surprised to see small bunches of tiny white flowers raised on slender 3 ft. stems. Individually they may not be very impressive but grouped in places where there is little else to outshine them, perhaps hovering among hostas, they lift the scene unexpectedly.

Any reasonably retentive soil suits this plant, while full exposure to light produces the brightest colour. Once you have obtained a plant it can easily be increased, by division, in spring. It makes a root stock which creeps along the ground and can be separated into individual rooted pieces.

This *V. p.* 'Aurea' is related to *Centranthus ruber*, generally known as Red Valerian which is a most accommodating plant and will grow almost anywhere short of waterlogged soil. It is often naturalized on crumbling ruins or stony banks. Old plants form a woody base which sprouts fresh, growth-making, large plants about 3 ft. high, but if they are pruned to the base in spring, fresher, tidier plants are formed. They produce long flower stems clustered with minute, deep pink flowers which make a cottage garden show for weeks in midsummer. Sometimes a white form will appear among a batch of seedlings.

Valeriana phu 'Aurea'

Hacquetia epipactis

Hacquetia epipactis

This is not a commonly grown plant, but for those who know it it is as much treasured as the first aconite, unharmed by inevitable late frosts, yet remaining a feature for weeks, unlike the aconites which are faded all too soon. *Hacquetia epipactis* can scarcely wait to get its buds through the bare soil before it opens wide its unusual green flowers. In shape they somewhat resemble a broad-petalled daisy, 1–2 inches across. In reality the six olive-green 'petals' are really bracts which draw attention to the cluster of tiny yellow twinkling flowers which fill the centre. As the weeks go by more and more buds open, until by April you have a low mound of flowers 4–5 inches high which makes a surprisingly bright accent. The flowers come so thick and fast they smother the shining, deeply divided leaves; but as they fade the leaves remain a neat low background for something else. This plant used to be called *Dondia epipactis*, and its petal-like bracts remind me of the astrantias or masterworts, to which it is related.

Possibly if it were in flower in mid summer this quaint plant might be overlooked, but any plant which shows flowers or good foliage in March will extend the time you can enjoy your garden. Although most trees and shrubs will be leafless, and much of the soil bare, there is already a feeling of life fermenting just beneath the surface. Tiny new shoots are emerging every day, buds are swelling, a faint haze of green has suddenly spread over the weeping willows, while the clean strong shoots of *Hemerocallis* repeat the lively yellow-green of *Hacquetia*. Both set off scattered drifts of the tiny, sky-blue Grape Hyacinth, *Muscari azureum*, which is prettier and much less troublesome than the commonly grown *Muscari botryoides*.

Hacquetia epipactis is found wild in bushy places in the eastern Alps. In the garden a cool pocket of deep soil in the rock garden, or on the edge of a border in semi-shade where the soil is reasonably retentive, is the kind of site which suits it. It makes slowly increasing clumps with a root system which looks like a bundle of black boot laces. They should be planted in the dormant season, as pot-grown plants or as seedlings since they can resent disturbance.

Several Kinds of Daphne

On a mild day in March the garden can be drenched with the rich scent of *Daphne odora* 'Aureomarginata'. (The last bit means that its neat, oval, evergreen leaves are faintly edged with cream.)

Reserve the warmest site in the garden for this powerful treasure. In good deep soil, with its back to a south wall, it greets you every spring with the sweetest and freshest of scents, warmer than lemon, but no less fresh.

It grows slowly. In twenty years it may be 4 ft. across and about $2\frac{1}{2}$ ft. high. Beneath its tidy canopy of leaves dense branches divide and subdivide while every smallest twig is topped with a rosette of smooth, leathery leaves, in the centre of which sits a tight cluster of purplish-pink buds. Gradually they open into small, cream, wax-like flowers stained with pink. *D. odora* does not set seed in the garden; it is usually grown from cuttings.

Flowering at the same time, with a different more spicey perfume, is the well-known *D. mezereum*, which can be grown almost anywhere, with its head in the sun and its roots in the shade. Making a smaller more upright bush, the little flowers, in purplish-red or white, are set in groups of two or three all along the bare twigs before the leaves appear. The fertilized flowers set currant-sized berries, yellow for the white flowers, red for the pink. They say that the hard seed inside must pass through the stomach of a bird before it will germinate. We try to reach the ripe berries before the birds and put them into a jampot filled with water to stand until they ferment. (The smell becomes disgusting.) Then we sow them. Sometimes the germination is quite good. If it is not we leave the pans for a second year, when usually more appear.

For several years I grew *D.* 'Somerset'. It formed quite quickly a large, beautifully shaped dome more than 4 ft. across and about 3 ft. high. In May and June it was smothered with pale pink, deliciously scented blossoms. However, due to some upheaval (inevitable as gardens mature and expand) it had to go, but somehow I must find a place for it again.

I have not mentioned *D. cneorum*, the famous Garland Flower which is found clustered against sun warmed boulders in the central and southern Alps, as I do not grow it. It is not an easy plant to establish. However I have no problems with *D. collina*. This is the perfect small shrub to dominate an area of small-scale planting, being full of character, yet only about 18 inches high and across, respectably covered with small, dark, evergreen leathery leaves. Each tip shoot carries a cluster of scented, rosy-purple flowers in May, and will continue to produce a few more throughout the summer, at the same time setting a fine crop of conspicuous orange fruits.

Daphne odora 'Aureomarginata'

Epimedium × versicolor 'Sulphureum'

Epimediums

I think that epimediums are not nearly as well known as they deserve to be. Imagine crowded clumps of slender stems, about a foot high, carrying dainty sprays of tiny, columbine-shaped flowers (without the long spurs), in delicate shades of lemon, soft lilac, deep rose and white. They are quickly followed, and indeed engulfed, by the beautiful foliage which remains attractive and, above all, is invaluable as ground-cover for the rest of the year. Some of them retain their leaves throughout winter but these must be cut off by March at the latest or you will never see those enchanting little flowers.

The roots are tough and fibrous while leaf stalks emerge from a tangled mat of underground stems. The exceptionally pretty leaves are a gift to gardeners and flower-arrangers. Heart-shaped, held in groups of three on thin, wiry stems, they are perhaps most attractive in April and May when their soft green base colour is overlaid and marbled with warm bronze deepening to brick red. They vary in form. In some the leaves may be smaller, their spring colour almost milk-chocolate in colour. As the leaves mature, by June, the colour will have changed, becoming almost uniformly green, but the fine mounds of overlapping leaves allow no possibility of weeds seeding among them.

Epimediums are related to the Berberis family and will grow in sun, in retentive soil, but do best in shade or part shade in soil with leaf mould.

There are several species found growing wild throughout Europe and Asia, and from them good garden hybrids have arisen. All epimediums increase rather slowly but *Epimedium × versicolor* 'Sulphureum' is one of the more robust, with larger leaves and delicate pale yellow flowers. *E. × rubrum* has the most brilliantly red marbled leaves in April and May, with small crimson flowers.

I value the truly evergreen forms which remain handsome in winter, bright green and fresh among leaf-litter and ferns.

From Germany has come a selected clone of *E. perralderianum* called 'Fronleiten'. Its new leaves are warmly tinted with reddish marbling, maturing to glossy green while bright canary-yellow flowers are held on long sprays above the leaves in May.

Dwarf Prunuses

Throughout the winter and early spring months I have watched my bushes of Dwarf Russian Almond, *Prunus tenella* (*Amygdalus nanus*) to make sure their buds were not being stripped by hungry bullfinches. Deep rose-tinted buds crowd multitudes of thin leafless stems creating bouquet-like masses of clear pink blossoms. This shrub is inclined to wander. If you have space you can allow a little colony to develop, if not then you must chop off the suckering shoots and give them away. Blue flowered bulbs, such as *Muscari* or *Scilla*, look enchanting scattered beneath them, or the double white *Arabis* will sweep through a sea of white froth, as well as making useful ground-cover among the thin wandering stems.

Prunus triloba (*Triloba* 'Multiplex') is sturdier in growth, and taller, about 4–5 ft. If pruned the previous season, slim and unbranched wands will be produced, wreathed in April with fat, deep-rose buds, opening flat, shell-pink double flowers whose centres are speckled with curling white stamens, buttoned together with a green eye.

Both these shrubs need hard pruning immediately after flowering. If you never prune the result will be a thicket of old wood carrying only short twigs of blossom. Take your courage and your secateurs and cut back the shoots of faded flowers to a basal framework. There will already be new growth shoots formed on these old flowering shoots, about 4–5 inches long. They will be very soft, but if you put them under a mist propagator many of them will take root.

My bushes of *P. triloba* are on their own roots, grown in deep retentive soil, in an open border. They flower and grow well, which is not always the case with grafted specimens. Some commercial nurseries supply bushes which are rooted from cuttings, but many offer bushes which have been grafted. These can be troublesome with shoots suckering from the stock.

Another small, bush-sized flowering cherry is at its best when these two have faded. *P. glandulosa* 'Alba Plena' is an enchanting sight when its pure white, double flowers wreath the slender twiggy branches which are already furnished with a setting of tiny fresh green leaves. There is a bright pink form of this, with double flowers, called *P. g.* 'Sinensis'. Both can be cut and brought into a warm room to open sprays of blossom weeks before they would open in the garden.

Prunus triloba

Erythronium 'White Beauty'

Erythroniums

On a sunny day, in the latter half of March, nothing is more exciting than to come upon well-grown clusters of *Erythronium dens-canis* which is the proper name for this well-loved member of the Lily family, better known as Dog's Tooth Violet. Dog's Tooth refers to the small, pointed and polished, ivory-white corms which you will find clustered beneath the soil when the leaves of an established clump have died away. The flowers are not remotely like violets, much more like elegant cyclamens, poised and fluttering like trapped butterflies above the exquisite foliage. Of cool, almost wax-like texture, broadly oval in shape, the young leaves are irregularly marbled in deep chocolate-brown and fresh light green. The long slender flower buds, on 5-inch naked stems, point earthwards until a warm ray of sunshine unfolds them, then they fly backwards like pointed wings, leaving the blue powdered stamens and white stigma exposed. The flowers are generally warm cyclamen-pink, but they can be found in white and rose-pink. *E. dens-canis* is the only European and Asian species, and can be naturalized in grass, or among shrubs. It is easily grown, preferably in part shade, and it likes a cool leaf mould or peaty soil.

To follow, in April, will come the American species. Usually found in mountain woods or on grassy slopes are several taller species in exquisite shades of cream, yellow and pink with descriptive names like Adder's Tongue and Glacier Lily. Most of them have a pair of large tongue-shaped shining leaves, often spotted or blotched like a thrush's breast.

Erythronium californicum has especially well-marked leaves, rich brown marbling over a jade green base. Above them stand slender stems 10–12 inches tall carrying several cream-coloured, lily-like flowers that look too fragile to stand up to the blistering east winds which usually bedevil our spring; but they grow, and increase most satisfactorily.

Two superb hybrids well known in gardens are *E.* 'Pagoda', and *E.* 'White Beauty'. Tallest is *E.* 'Pagoda', with 15–18 inch branching stems carrying several rich butter-yellow lily-like flowers, while *E.* 'White Beauty' has paler, cream-coloured flowers. The large, shining, tongue-shaped leaves are slightly mottled brown, like snakeskin. By June all trace of leaves will have vanished, only seed pods remaining.

Erythroniums take several years to flower from seed. Named varieties must be obtained as corms. After several years one corm will have produced a cluster of offsets. These can be lifted when the leaves have died down and replanted to create natural looking drifts along the edges of shady walks. They will grow in sun or part shade, but last longer where sheltered.

Small Anemones

It is impossible to select one favourite spring anemone when there are so many.

Anemone blanda produces sheets of many petalled flowers, in shades of pink and blue, but there is also a magnificent white form, called 'White Splendour'. These dainty plants make quite large, underground, woody rhizomes which you can cut up when the leaves have died down to increase your stock. They also seed freely and will naturalize themselves along the edge of a sunny border provided there are not too many smothering weeds.

For shady gardens there are several forms of *Anemone nemorosa*, our native Wood Anemone. This will spread freely in shady conditions, in friable soil, full of decayed vegetable matter. Good forms include the double white *A. n.* 'Vestal' which produces tight little Victorian posies. Best of all are lovely lilac-blue forms. These make exquisite, shallow, saucer-shaped flowers, much larger than the commonly seen single white. They open flat to the sun to show a central mass of yellow stamens. One of the best named blue forms is *A. n.* 'Robinsoniana'.

Anemone pulsatilla, now called *Pulsatilla vulgaris*, is the Pasque flower, Flower of Easter. Preferring full sun in well-drained soil, it makes a tidy nest of finely cut leaves, in which nestles a clutch of silken hair-covered buds, that slowly unfold wide to the sun soft violet-purple petals filled with yellow stamens. There is a white form covered with fine silvery down. The gauzy globes of seed heads which follow are no less attractive.

Anemone pavonina, found wild in southern Europe, revels in sunny places, in light or heavy soil. Seedlings produce flowers up to 3 inches across on 12-inch stems in almost all shades of the rainbow: white, pale coral, deep rose-red, scarlet and soft lavender-purple, all with remarkable centres filled with navy-blue stamens. They flower throughout March and April, and are easy and reliable perennials.

Continuing the season is *A. magellanica* whose pale, primrose-yellow flowers are followed by bantam egg-sized seed pods. These explode when ripe into large, creamy, cotton wool-like cocoons in which the seeds are protected and dispersed.

All these anemones can be grown from seed provided it is sown when ripe, usually in mid-summer, and just lightly covered with grit.

—35—

Pulsatilla vulgaris

Fritillaria meleagris

Fritillaries

April is the month for fritillaries. First come the great crown-heads of Crown Imperials, *Fritillaria imperialis*, with large burnt-orange or citron-yellow bells topped with tufts of leaves like a pineapple. Everything from the huge, grapefruit-sized bulbs, the thick stems set with whorls of glistening green leaves to the flowers themselves, has a strongly pungent smell, offensive to some; they say it smells like foxes, but for me the first time I catch the scent as it drifts across the garden on a mild day I know that spring has come, and I look around for the fat noses pushing through the soil. The stems rush up, seeming to grow inches a day, until they stand 3 ft. and more tall, exceedingly handsome grown in clumps in a large border, or among shrubs.

Far less showy but with sinister charm is our own Snakes-Head Fritillary, *F. meleagris*. It stands about 12–15 inches tall with drooping heads of dark, chequered purple, overlaid with a greyish bloom. Sometimes you find white ones with faint green chequering, others may be light plum coloured. They like rich, heavy soil, and will have disappeared by July, except for the attractive seed heads.

There are many more fritillaries. They come mostly in quiet colours, but are so distinctive. *F. pyrenaica* from the Pyrenees, is one of the easiest to grow in well-drained, enriched soil, in a sunny situation. Its drooping bells are dark, matt chocolate-brown, perfectly contrasted with enamelled green linings which just show as the edge of the petals roll slightly upwards.

Fritillaria pallidiflora, found wild in central Siberian mountains, is a great treasure with large, pale, lemon-yellow bells, several to a stem when grown well in rich soil.

Fritillaria camtschatcensis also demands good soil in part shade. Its fresh-green, glossy leaves are set in whorls round the stem, looking not unlike lilies emerging, but the flower stems (12–15 inches tall) carry open, pendant bells which are smooth and almost black outside, heavily corrugated inside where the colour is slightly warmer, dark chocolate-maroon.

None of these fritillaries is gaudy; but it is worth waiting all the year round to marvel again at their mysterious beauty.

All fritillaries can be grown from seed. The large ones take up to 7 years to flower, the smaller ones 3–4 years. If your Crown Imperials do not flower give them a top dressing of well-rotted farmyard manure. Or dig them up when dormant, prepare better fed holes (they might be over-crowded), replant them, and wait a year or so for them to build larger bulbs.

Dwarf Periwinkles

The weed-smothering carpets of the Dwarf Periwinkle, *Vinca minor*, do a splendid job by covering some of the poorest soil in the garden. It is a much better garden plant than the unruly *V. major*, except for the beautiful variegated form, *V. major* 'Variegata' ('Elegantissima').

All forms of *V. minor* flower well, but the finest is 'Bowles' Variety'. Its creeping stems set with small, shining, evergreen leaves cover the soil in sun or shade, rooting as they go. Embroidered over this living carpet are clustered knots or trailing stems of bold silk-textured flowers of rich lavender-blue. There is a fine plum-red form called 'Punicea', while 'Multiplex' has double rows of smaller petals in a slightly paler shade of plum. Paler and smaller too is the double blue called 'Caerulea Plena'. There is a tantalizing myth that a double white exists in some secret garden.

My favourite white form, *V. minor* 'Alba', not only produces an abundance of flowers but also has very attractive foliage, being variegated in light and dark green. *V. m.* 'Variegata' has cream and green leaves with light blue flowers whose petals are more widely spaced, creating a starry effect against the pale background.

My love for these plants increased dramatically when I learnt to use a mulch among them. Previously much time and temper had been wasted fiddling out weed seedlings from among the trailing runners. By covering the bare soil between the plants with at least an inch layer of coarse peat, or crushed bark, the majority of germinating seedlings are stifled. The long trailing shoots root quickly into the mulch and in two years create their own soil protection so that little additional mulching is needed.

Dwarf periwinkles will grow in any soil short of bog, in sun or shade. They are ideal for covering rough banks or carpeting the soil among shrubs, or in light woodland. In my garden all the different forms of *V. minor* make a tidy evergreen edge along a curving drive where bulbs such as snowdrops and daffodils in spring, and colchicums in autumn, come up through them. They are trimmed occasionally to encourage fresh growth.

Vinca difformis is a treasure for warmer gardens than mine. I saw it in full flower in February in southern Ireland climbing through netting fixed to a toolshed wall. From a distance I was drawn to a cascade of white blossom. It is usually described as being milky-blue.

Vinca minor

Primula auricula, in variety

Primula auricula

What exotic, sumptuously rich-looking flowers are the auriculas ('them reckless plants' as an old country friend of mine used to call them). Whether you have a batch of plants grown from seed, or grow named and famed varieties, every one is worth having.

Primula auricula, which grows in the European Alps, will grow in full sun provided it has sufficiently rich soil, but it will not tolerate bad drainage, nor wet around the crown. A top dressing of gravel or chippings around the stem and beneath the leaves will help both from rotting. Then, most satisfyingly and with the minimum of attention they will produce healthy-looking rosettes of leaves. Some may be plain green, others will be heavily coated with white meal, looking as lovely as flowers themselves.

The generous, many-headed clusters of flowers are to be found in every hue, from deepest burgundy-black through shades of purple, blue and red to soft lilac, pinky-buff and various yellows. They may have large eyes in yellowy-green or ivory-white, or have scarcely an eye at all. The texture of the petals is often thick and velvety, frilled at the edges, sometimes bell-shaped, but more often wide-eyed open. A low round pot filled with a mixed bunch of these flowers, including a few double forms is an entrancing sight. In the garden they are easy to grow and last well; not to be confused with the famous show auriculas which need glass protection.

Among the famous the named varieties are 'Old Yellow Dusty Miller', and 'Old Red Dusty Miller', both with white mealy leaves. These two do not increase as freely as some other varieties and because they can only be reproduced by division they tend to be rather more scarce.

Primula marginata is another mountain crevice plant, from the Maritime Alps. It makes rather smaller rosettes of leaves which are dusted with creamy-gold farina, with prettily cut edges, so fine and even as though they had been cut out with pinking shears. Clustered heads of cool-lavender flowers usually open before the auriculas have thought to stir themselves. Selected forms have been named, some have larger flowers in darker, or lighter shades; in others those tooth-edged leaves are accentuated by silvery-white farina.

Water Irises

Iris pseudacorus is the proper name of our native Water Iris (commonly called Yellow Flag), still to be seen along riversides or pond edges. It makes huge clumps of luxuriant, dark green, broad-bladed leaves, and may be found either along the boggy edge, or in several inches of water. It is, however, an adaptable plant and will grow very successfully in gardens, in stiff retentive soil.

The form most valued is *I. p.* 'Variegata'. In late spring the young leaf blades are pale cream and buttery-yellow as they push through the straw-coloured curling remains of last years' leaves. By May they make vivid accents among the flood of rich green foliage all around. My favourite group has, at its base, the large Lady's Smock, *Cardamine latifolia*, whose floppy stems, carrying rich mauve flower heads, wreath in and out among the pale carved leaves of the Iris, forming a memorable picture.

By mid-June the great clumps (3–4 ft. tall) appear bicoloured. The mature leaves have become dark green, only the young leaves still thrusting up alongside are vivid pea-green. Rich yellow flowers appear above the leaves throughout June, and by the end of the month the leaves will be entirely green.

Iris pseudacorus 'Bastardii' has plain green leaves but the flowers are very pale lemon-yellow, well formed, with soft brown veining leading into the heart of the flower.

Neither of these forms should be allowed to seed because their offspring will not be true, and if allowed to develop will overpower the selected forms before you have noticed what is happening. In the small garden they add great style to an artificial pool when planted in a large container, just submerged.

Another iris which loves to be in shallow water is *I. laevigata* 'Variegata'. It is perhaps the best of the variegated water irises since it retains its bright colour throughout the growing season. The short fans of green leaves are vividly striped with ivory-white.

Iris laevigata produces a generous mass of soft green leaves which makes a good background for sheaves of lavender-blue flowers, recognizable by their broad drooping falls. 'Alba' is a very fine white form. 'Rose Queen' is a hybrid with *I. kaempferi* so is less tolerant of waterlogged soil. Its soft old-rose flowers are very unusual.

All these forms of *I. laevigata* will grow in full sun, in soil which remains moist.

Iris pseudacorus 'Variegatus'

Arabis caucasica

Some Less Common Arabises

Cushions of white *Arabis, Arabis caucasica* (*A. albida*), together with carpets of purple *Aubrieta* are as much part of the April garden as sunshine and showers. There are two other varieties of *Arabis* which I like very much. *A. c.* 'Variegata' is handsome all the year round. Even in winter its low neat rosettes of felt-textured, grey-green leaves, boldly margined with creamy-white, stand out against the bare soil. But by mid-April they disappear for several weeks beneath a froth of creamy-white blossoms floating on 8-inch stems. My favourite perhaps, is the double-flowered variety, *A. c.* 'Flore Pleno'. In the early stages leaves, buds and stems have a slight purplish flush which faintly tints the opening petals. As the stems lengthen the spires of ivory-white flowers remind me of tiny double stocks. Lovely to pick for small arrangements, the plants quickly make good ground-cover on the edge of a sunny, well-drained border.

Arabis causica 'Rosabella' makes neater, low-growing mats of foliage with short-stemmed clusters of cyclamen-pink flowers which fade to paler pink.

Arabis ferdinandi-coburgii, in spite of such a cumbersome name, is another all-the-year-round delight. Much more daintily constructed than *A. caucasica* it is ideal for the rock garden, or raised bed. Very small rosettes of narrow, shining, green and white variegated leaves press themselves into flat carpets against the soil. Throughout April they carry fluttering stems of tiny white flowers. There are several other forms of *Arabis* which can be found in the Alpine Garden Society's seed list. Selected forms including variegated plants must be propagated by division or cuttings.

In recent years my plants of *A. caucasica* have suffered attack by the arabis midge which lays its eggs among the leaf buds causing a compact gall to form in which hatch out pinkish-white maggots. The effect is depressing — only a few malformed flowering shoots and small weakly side shoots — instead of the normal wealth of blossom followed by a carpet of strong healthy rosettes. Regular treatment with nicotine dust will eventually destroy the successive generations of maggots if you feel you cannot use a systemic insecticide.

Euphorbias

Euphorbia is commonly known as Spurge, or Milkweed. The *Euphorbia* genus includes plants which outshine almost every other plant in the garden; even the most flamboyant reds cannot subdue my plants of *E. wulfenii*. Their huge cylindrical heads are made up of hundreds of closely packed saucer-shaped discs arranged in a fascinating spiral pattern, and are of a peculiarly luminous shade of yellow-green which stands out like a light among all the thousand shades of new spring green.

This amazing plant opens its first flowers in a mild February, and will still be handsome in June when its seed pods are popping. Then you cut off the old flowering stems at the base to make way for new shoots clothed in whorls of narrow blue-green leaves which will carry next year's flowers. A well-grown plant may have 20 or 30 stems standing 4 ft. and more high. They are easy to grow in most gardens, preferring a sunny, well-drained site sheltered from icy winds which can kill them or leave them looking like dejected hens with bedraggled feathers. Strangely it seems, young plants are rarely damaged.

For gardens that might feel overpowered by these big bush-like plants there are several smaller cousins with perhaps even more brilliantly greenish-yellow flower heads. *E. polychroma* is one of these, producing scores of stems about 15 inches high, topped with yellow heads which catch the eye no less than daffodils but last for weeks longer.

For cooler soil and situations there is a spurge called *E. griffithii* 'Fireglow', which stands about 3 ft. high and astounds you with flat-topped heads of bright tomato-red, toned down with red veined leaves which have an almost brown or olive tone to soften the savage colour.

Euphorbia amygdaloides is our native Wood Spurge, sometimes seen in copsy places or hedge bottoms. A fine selected form called 'Purpurea' has leaves and stems strongly tinted purplish-red. The colour is brightest in winter and early spring, draining as the leaves mature to dark blue-green.

Another woodland *Euphorbia* which pleases all the year round is *E. robbiae*. Tolerant of dry shade, it will grow in sun or shade in any soil that is not waterlogged. Dense colonies of large, dark green leaf rosettes make lively looking ground-cover in winter, and are lit for weeks in spring and early summer with long heads of yellowish-green flowers, but are susceptible to damage in cold districts.

There are many more euphorbias to suit all conditions. *E. palustris* makes a lovely sight in completely soggy soil.

Euphorbia wulfenii

Erysimum linifolium 'Bowles' Mauve'

Erysimum linifolium 'Bowles' Mauve'

When I stoop to put my face into the velvet-textured, crumpled petals of old-fashioned wallflowers and smell the rich heavy scent I feel almost unbearably sad — the kind of feeling evoked only by reminders of childhood. I still enjoy seeing them mixed up with tulips and the pheasant-eyed narcissus, but in my own garden I grow several other perennial wallflowers.

My favourite is *Erysimum linifolium* 'Bowles' Mauve'. It does not look in the least like the common wallflower, neither does it have any haunting perfume. But that omission is completely outweighed by the plant's extra-ordinary performance. Two years ago I planted a young rooted cutting at the base of a south-facing wall. Now it is a dense, rounded bush, 4 ft. across and 3 ft. high, clothed to the ground in neat rosettes of narrow, dark, grey-green leaves, held on a stiff framework of stems. Each mature shoot carries a flower stem up to 12 inches tall, closely set with small, tidy, four-petalled flowers. The colour effect is enhanced by the unopened buds at the tip of the stems which are darkest purple. They open to lilac but lower down the stem become light vibrant purple. What is remarkable is the length of time these flower spikes last. Nor is that all. Successive waves of side-shoots continue to produce new spikes of flowers indefinitely; nothing short of winter frost deters them. Sometimes I feel I must take pity on my plants and cut off some of the flowers to give them a rest.

As this plant does not set seed it must be propagated from cuttings. These can be taken almost any time during the growing season. Look for young shoots which are firming nicely, but without formed flower buds. Although the parent plant will last in good heart for several years it will eventually lose its fresh vigour and need to be replaced with a young plant.

It is important to choose a good site, well protected from wind which will rock the plant and produce an ungainly lop-sided shape. If you nip out the flower shoot when first planted it will allow the plant to make a good shape and strong root system to support the wealth of flowers which will follow.

Another long-lived wallflower is *Cheiranthus cheiri* 'Harpur Crewe'. This makes a much smaller plant, usually not much more than a foot across, which carries short spires of neatly double flowers. They are yellow and sweetly scented.

The Pacific Coast Hybrid Irises

Some of the most exquisite of early summer flowers are found under this unwieldy title. So unlike the large ramrod-stiff clumps of familiar border irises, these little hybrids are orchid-like in daintiness and delicacy of form and colour. They are only one step from being as found in the wild: natural hybrids between several species found along the seaboard of North California, growing on grassy banks, or in clearings in pine forests, relishing fairly rich soil, and not stinted of rainfall.

In the garden they make low tussocky clumps of evergreen grassy leaves which themselves provide useful ground-cover along the edge of a border. In May, long slender flower stems appear from among the rose-tinted leaf bases, carrying flights of flowers like butterflies. Long, furled and pointed buds open silk-textured petals, frilled and ruffled in every pastel shade imaginable. Almost all are intricately veined with fine dark pencilling. Some are self-coloured, that is, the same colour all over, in shades of blue or yellow. Others may be orchid-pink with white, or bronzed-tan with yellow. Some of the blues and lilacs are toned and shadowed as the light shines through the petals — I have a grey-blue one which seems to match the rain clouds on a summer's day. They last in flower for several weeks. Not until autumn do you pay much attention to their dark arching foliage. Then suddenly among the leaves you notice seed pods splitting open to form a shape as attractive as flowers, crinkled brown outside, pale cream within. On dried and curving stems they make something special for winter arrangements.

One of the parents of these hybrid irises, *Iris innominata*, was introduced in 1935 from Oregon. It usually produces deep golden flowers delicately veined with brown and buff. In the wild it is found in all shades from pale cream and apricot to orchid-pink and deep blue-purple. It has very narrow grassy leaves.

Iris douglasiana, another parent, is a very robust plant, with broader, longer leaves, making larger heavier clumps, with handsome rose-red staining at the base of the leaves. The usual colour of the flowers is blue or purplish.

Good drainage is essential for all these irises. They will grow in full sun or part shade in soil that has been enriched with humus. Generally speaking they prefer a lime-free soil, but *I. douglasiana* will tolerate some lime, and does not object to salt spray. It is generally advised that the division of clumps of specially good hybrids is best done immediately after flowering, shortening the leaves at the same time.

—43—

Iris innominata hybrids

Rheum palmatum 'Atrosanguineum'

Ornamental Rhubarbs

One of the most dramatic of garden plants is the ornamental rhubarb, *Rheum palmatum*. Placed in a bay among shrubs, or used to break the monotony of a border, this noble plant can transform a competent, but not inspired, piece of planting.

There are several forms. Perhaps the most striking is *R. p.* 'Atrosanguineum'. Large, cherry-red buds burst from the scaly, woody root stocks towards the end of March. Quite quickly the young leaves unfold, crumpled, their colour dark reddish-purple on the top side, much lighter on the reverse side. As the leaves expand the surface colour fades to bronze green; beneath, colour is retained. A light breeze ruffling the great mounds of deeply cut leaves reveals the bright colour like a glimpse of coloured petticoats. By the end of May tall stout stems (6 ft.) carry large fluffy heads of tiny crimson flowers.

There are several variations of the red-leafed rhubarb. I have one which is even more noble, *R. p. tanguticum*, with larger leaves, more richly coloured; but its flowers are surprisingly white. Another form which I covet is *R. atropurpureum dissectum* whose reddish-purple leaves are deeply cut.

Where there is already much colour in the garden I think the cool apple-green form of *R. palmatum* is preferable. It tends to be overlooked when the two are compared in isolation. But in many plantings its grand piles of huge, less intricately divided leaves fit more quietly, yet no less importantly, into the design. These plants need to be sheltered from tearing winds, in deep well-enriched soil, in sun or part shade. Waterlogged soil will cause the great starchy crowns to rot.

Rheum alexandrae, from Tibet and N.W. China, is quite different from these ornamental rhubarbs. On short stems it forms clusters of much smaller heart-shaped leaves with pale parallel veins standing out against dark shining green. In June, a $2\frac{1}{2}$ – 3 ft. flower spike emerges, set from top to bottom with large, pale cream, overlapping papery bracts beneath which are hidden little clusters of typical rhubarb flowers, sheltering from the mountain rainstorms which they expect in China. Unfortunately these unique, pagoda-like structures are infrequently produced in cultivation. They do best in cool, moist climates.

Rheum nobile is from Nepal and is similar, although even less amenable to cultivation. The bracts grow to 1 ft. in width in the wild.

Alliums

For many people the bulb season ends with tulips; but various members of the onion family provide us with interesting flowers until late summer. By the end of May some of the most showy ones are decorating my grey and silver garden, standing well above the mounds of scented santolina and lavender.

Allium aflatunense looks very like the domestic onion gone to seed, but its round head, poised on 3-ft. stems, is tightly packed with deep lavender-coloured flowers. Much more curious, and quite different, is *A. bulgaricum*, found wild in the Balkans. Tall, thick stems are topped with flowers encased in papery envelopes, like pointed candle snuffers, which split open to release a dangling head of large open bells with thick wax-textured petals. They are palest cream, overlaid with olive green, and touched with deep plum-red inside, which glows faintly through the translucent petals. As they are fertilized the flowers turn upwards eventually to form straw-coloured pointed seed heads.

Most alliums smell rather unpleasant when bruised or cut, but once arranged do not scent the room. There are many more, varying in shapes and shades from tight-packed, plum-sized heads of deep wine to open airy globes almost as large as a football.

Not the least decorative is *A. schoenoprasum*, better known as chives. The best form is *A. s. sibiricum* with larger leaves for the kitchen and masses of pinky-mauve flowers, pretty to look at and good to eat, broken up and sprinkled over salads.

Almost as large as a football is the amazing flower head of *A. christophii*, found wild in the Kopet Dagh mountains, on the borders of north Iran. It is a marvellous design of strength and delicacy. A short stem, about 18 inches high, carries an immense head of glistening lilac stars with petals touching tip to tip, to form a huge, airy globe about 10 inches across. It dries in perfect shape, the delicate spoke-like stems which support the bleached head remaining purple.

Almost all alliums form good seed heads. If picked before they have been beaten and blackened by wind and wet weather they will retain their beautiful sculptured shapes and pale straw colour throughout the winter.

Alliums like a fairly rich soil, in full sun. They can be grown from seed, the larger flowered ones taking several years to blossom.

Allium christophii and *A. bulgaricum*

Geum × *intermedium* 'Coppertone'

Dwarf Geums

Geum rivale, Water Avens, is a British native and is sometimes found in low-lying damp meadows. The selected form usually grown in gardens is called 'Leonard's Variety', and it is a most endearing plant. It spreads weed-smothering clumps of healthy, dark green, divided leaves slowly over any cold dim spot which, in May, will be quietly illuminated by a profusion of drooping bell-shaped flowers. It will flower in sun if the soil remains damp. The soft coppery-pink petals are overlaid with pointed mahogany-red calyces, while the slender, dark tinted stems (standing 12–15 inches high) are bowed over at the tips by the gentle weight of flowers.

Geum rivale 'Lionel Cox' is similar, but its flowers of greenish-yellow are more open with rather crinkled petals and shorter stems. This plant looks best on the edge of a border, in good retentive soil, in sun or part shade.

Very cool and modest is *G. r.* 'Album' with white flowers drooping from pale green calyces. Another small example which makes a good edging plant is *G.* 'Borisii'. Neat clumps of leaves form a perfect setting for the upturned flowers of brilliant tomato-red, their centres filled with orange stamens.

A robust *Geum* which is fine for quickly filling in gaps is called *G.* × *intermedium*. For weeks it carries a display of bright yellow flowers on interlacing thin brown stems, while the reddish-brown sepals and hairy centres remain long after the petals have dropped. A seedling from this plant occurred in my garden, with slightly nodding flowers of a colour hard to describe — a soft apricot-pink, or maybe the colour of newly polished copper — so we called it 'Coppertone'.

I have two other geums which comfortably suit dampish pockets in the rock garden. *G. montanum*, found wild in mountain meadows or open woods in the Alps, is a gem. In deep cool soil it produces large, cupped, yellow flowers, mostly in early summer, but a few more appear later in the year. Just as attractive are the feathery, globular seed heads in warm rusty-brown. Generous clumps of rounded, softly hairy leaves create a feeling of well being. There is a form, *G. m.* 'Maximum', collected in the Eastern Alps which is even more splendid, with extra large flowers on slightly taller stems. Alas, I have not seen it.

Geum rossii has interesting foliage. It makes tight clumps of deeply cut greyish-green leaves which surround the short bouquet of bright yellow flowers like a Victorian posy frill.

Apart from the vivid 'Borisii' all these geums have an agreeable softness of colour which suits the tender greens of early summer, and none of them needs unsightly staking, as do the larger double flowered hybrids.

Wild Paeonies

You do not often see single-flowered paeonies in gardens, the excuse usually being that they do not last. This is true for most of them but I have one which gives me pleasure for several weeks towards the end of May and into the first weeks of June. It is called *Paeonia veitchii*, having been collected in China by the firm of Veitch.

I think plants should be judged for their overall effect, not just for their large and impressive flower heads which may flop untidily because you have forgotten to stake them in time. *P. veitchii* needs no staking. It makes neat mounds of fresh green, lightly dissected foliage which is itself an attraction all summer. Above it are poised a succession of delicate flowers, slightly nodding, reminiscent in shape of large single roses, with silk-textured petals, slightly fluted and frilled. In colour they can be found in all shades of pink, from soft magenta through blushing rose to white, each filled with a centre of golden stamens. Seen all together it is difficult to pick a favourite, but the almost white form, warmed with the palest wash of pink, I perhaps like best. The flowers vary in size, the largest being about 3–4 inches across. Each slender stem carries two or three buds which prolong the display.

Almost as attractive are the seed pods in autumn. Small and fat, they split open to show pearl-sized glistening blue seeds set against crinkled red linings. They are easily grown in sun or part shade, in light or heavy soils. Grown from seed they will take about 3 or 4 years to flower.

Paeonia mlokosewitschii is usually over by the end of May, but has already decorated the garden since the end of February when fat, cherry-red buds are seen breaking through the soil. Slowly they unfold leaves of a beautiful, indescribable shade, a warm brownish-maroon which gradually fades to soft grey-green as the flower buds swell in early May. It is worth the whole year's waiting to see delicate lemon-yellow petals open to filtered sunlight, sheltering in their hearts a mass of golden stamens which surround the cherry-coloured stigma.

The beauty of these lovely flowers is short lived, but a carefully chosen position, sheltered from bright sun and wind, helps to retain their perfection a little longer. Like *P. veitchii* they draw attention to themselves in autumn with large fat seed pods which suddenly split open to show the same brilliant crimson lining, and sloe-black seeds.

Sow these seeds, and expect to wait five years at least before you will have flowering plants.

Paeonia veitchii

Polygonatum × *hybridum*

Solomon's Seal, and a Relation

What should we do, as gardeners or flower-arrangers, without Solomon's Seal, whether it be to create a little woodland effect with a few ferns, a hosta or two, and a shady site, or to provide throughout the summer arching stems of healthy foliage to make a frame for the large and imposing flower arrangement.

When you delve into the subject you find there are several different kinds. Most commonly grown is *Polygonatum* × *hybridum* (*P. multiflorum* of gardens). Being a hybrid this can vary in size of leaf and length of stem. Left undisturbed for several years, in a cool shaded spot, it will make a luxurious stand of graceful stems set along its entire length with elegantly poised, simple leaves, while beneath them hang little clusters of greeny-white bells. I have a smaller leafed variation which sets handsome clusters of greenish-black berries, but have not yet discovered its true name.

There are two variations of variegated Solomon's Seal. *P.* × *hybridum* 'Variegatum' is a very scarce plant whose leaves are rather puckered by the fairly strong cream variegation which marks the edges and strays part way into the centres of the leaves. *P. falcatum* 'Variegatum' has only a slight cream edge to its smooth glossy leaves, but much better form. Both of these plants increase slowly, and they are never very plentiful as they can only be propagated by division.

Polygonatum verticillatum is also rarely seen and not much missed by most gardeners, but viewed isolated above lower plants it is, I think, a plant of character. Tall slender stems, up to 5 ft., make graceful columns set with whorls of long, narrow, pointed leaves. They diminish towards the top of the stems where clusters of tiny, drooping greenish-white bells form at the nodes. By the autumn these have become clusters of little red berries.

Smilacina racemosa is sometimes confused with Solomon's Seal which is its relation. The leaf shape is similar, but the habit rather more upright, while each stem is topped with a fluffy creamy-white spike of flowers having the freshest, sweetest scent imaginable. They say it sets berries, but although mine show promise they never stay the course. *Smilacina* requires lime-free soil. Both it and the polygonatums do best in cool situations, in retentive soil well laced with humus.

Several Crambes

I first encountered Sea Kale (*Crambe maritima*) as a vegetable. In February extra large pots or old buckets are placed over the knobbly crowns, with a piece of tile laid on top to keep out the light. The idea is to blanch the new shoots which are encouraged to spring up within the shelter. Some time in windy March you discover brittle ivory-coloured stems filling the container, topped with crumpled leaves which are tender shades of pink and cream and pewter grey. I used to cut these off and throw them away, eating only the stems which can be cooked and eaten like asparagus — simply delicious with butter. Then I found I could make a fresh spring salad with a bit of tarragon added to these crunchy titbits, at a time when anything delicate and raw is hard to find, except from the greenhouse.

I also value *C. maritima* highly for its ornamental effect. I plant it in strategic places along the edge of a border of sun and drought-loving plants. Placed in front of small-leafed plants such as artemisias, or tall feathery fennel, it creates a most handsome focal point. In March or April the emerging crinkled purple buds are a joy. By the end of May large heads of small creamy-white flowers stand just above the leaves which themselves create a bold feature until November frosts destroy them.

There is not another plant remotely like *C. maritima*. Its leaves are large and long with waved and scalloped edges. They loll sumptuously at the cut-grass edge, their fine sculptured form, with vivid wax-blue-green colouring, catching the eye as much as any bright flower.

Crambe cordifolia needs much more space. The basal mound is composed of huge, dark green leaves, rounded in shape and somewhat bristly. The flower shoots emerge as strong sturdy stems which soon divide and sub-divide to form a vast framework more than 6 ft. high which is enveloped in a cloud of tiny creamy-white flowers, honey-scented. This is a spectacular plant in large borders not bedevilled by strong winds which sometimes snap off these lovely heads when they are at their best.

I am glad to have discovered *C. koktebelica*. It is similar to *C. cordifolia* but on a much reduced scale. Standing only 3–4 ft. high its dainty heads of white flowers can add lightness nearer the front of a border.

All crambes like well-drained soil, situated in full sun. They can be propagated from root cuttings. In January or February take roots about the thickness of a pencil, not less, and cut them into 6-inch lengths and insert them in the soil so that the tops are scarcely covered. They can also be grown from seed.

Crambe maritima

Polemonium carneum

Jacob's Ladder

Polemonium caeruleum (Jacob's Ladder) is one of our oldest garden plants: it has been cultivated since Roman times. What a good thing it has not been abandoned in favour of something more fashionable! Its entire effect is pleasurable. Taking up only a modest amount of space it looks best where it has seeded among other lower plants, where its tallish stems (about $2\frac{1}{2}$ ft.), dressed in light green fern-like leaves, create a welcome break among soft rounded shapes. Each plant sends up several upright stems, and each stem carries, in a loose head, a long succession of shallow, saucer-shaped flowers whose rich blue petals have the texture of silk, the colour softened by sunlight filtered through them. A white form looks bewitching among cool green shadows.

Polemonium foliosissimum is similar, but has slightly longer and narrower leaflets, and the more cup-shaped flowers are held in denser clusters. They verge on the purple side of blue, so you might call it rich lilac. By the end of May the first flowers are opening, while, in my garden, I am astonished each year to see the same plants still producing flowers in October, among the velvet-red blossoms of *Lobelia cardinalis* 'Queen Victoria'.

Along a partly shaded walk I have a tumbled mass of *P. carneum*. Widely branched heads carry a wealth of flowers which open cream buds, becoming palest pink, then fading to soft lilac. They are larger than the flowers of either *P. caeruleum*, or *P. foliosissimum*. The dusky purple flowers of *Geranium phaeum*, or old-rose lockets of *Dicentra formosa* make good companions for this delicately lovely plant.

Provided you have retentive soil all these plants will grow in an open situation, but they look better, and last longer, where they do not endure the glare of the sun all day. They are not long-lived plants but can be rejuvenated by careful dividing in spring and then planting the pieces into fresh soil. They respond most satisfyingly to well-made garden compost.

Seeds will be freely produced so cut off spent flower heads if you wish to prolong the flowering season almost indefinitely. You will also save yourself the agony of destroying hundreds of healthy seedlings. One flower head allowed to go to seed and collected before the small, shining black seeds have dropped will give you far more plants than you will know what to do with.

Dwarf Campions

Lychnis viscaria, in its several forms, is a plant which cannot be called common, yet it makes such a tidy plant and produces such an abundance of flower that I wonder why it has not become as familiar as *Alyssum* or *Aubrieta*. It spends most of the year as a low, neat clump of narrow, dark green foliage; useful ground-cover if planted in close groups. Throughout June each clump produces a forest of stems, 12–15 inches high, carrying heads of close-set campion flowers in shocking magenta-pink. The stems have sticky patches between each node, hence the common name Sticky Campion. I presume this is to trap insects which must form some part of their diet.

Lychnis viscaria 'Alba' is the plant for those who are allergic to hot colours, its pure white flowers chilled by shadows from palest green calyces.

For some years I avoided the glowing descriptions in catalogues of *L. v.* 'Splendens Plena', as I was content with my single forms; but when eventually I saw this fine double form i could not resist it. It has taller stems, a good 2 ft. tall, with less densely packed heads of flower. But the individual flowers are much larger with rows of frilled and fluted thin-textured petals in a much brighter, rosier shade of pink. Among grey foliage plants, or blue flowered plants such as the low growing *Aster yunnanensis* 'Napsbury', which has large lavender-blue daisy flowers lit with warm orange centres, or grouped among the azure-blue Flax, *Linum perenne*, this plant is outstanding in its brilliance. But I would not be without the single forms which tend to flower earlier.

These plants are ideal as edge-of-the-border plants, in full sun, in any good garden soil. They can suffer in poor, dry, gravel soils, or in prolonged droughts.

A favourite little campion of mine which seems to survive in the driest of soil is *L. flos jovis*. Found wild in the central Alps on exposed rocky slopes and screes it seems quite at home in some of my worst gravel soil. I like its low tuffets of neat furry leaves which become almost white in summer heat and drought. The short branching stems (8–10 inches high), carrying small heads of rose-pink flowers, are a pleasure to meet, set among scented mats of thymes and groups of cobweb houseleeks.

Lychnis alpina 'Rosea' is smaller still and suitable for the raised bed or sink garden. Neat clusters of small, dark green leaves practically vanish beneath short stemmed heads of rich pink flowers.

Lychnis viscaria 'Splendens Plena'

Ranunculus aconitifolius 'Flore Pleno'

Double Buttercups

As small country children my friends and I loved to hold the glistening shallow bowls of field buttercups beneath each others chins to see the golden light reflected on our milk-pale skins. As adults we are less keen to see plants of Creeping Buttercup (*Ranunculus repens*) in our gardens where it rapidly becomes a smothering weed. However, there are in cultivation three forms of double-flowered buttercup, none of which is invasive.

The most prized is *R. aconitifolius* 'Flore Pleno', charmingly known as 'The Fair Maids of France'. Grown and cherished since the 16th century it remains a rare plant, increasing slowly, needing a cool moist soil. It makes a stiffly branching plant about $1\frac{1}{2}$ – 2 ft. high, carrying masses of small double white flowers, tinted green in the centre. The dark green, pointed foliage in no way detracts from the sense of lightness and space in which these perfectly formed blossoms float.

'Bachelor's Buttons' is the good country name for *R. acris* 'Flore Pleno', which was found in Lancashire, also in the 16th century. I cannot think why it is not seen more often in gardens today, being easily grown in full sun, in stiff retentive soil. It quickly makes strong clumps which produce slender stemmed bouquets ($2\frac{1}{2}$ – 3 ft.), crowded with small densely double flowers. It looks well with good forms of *Iris sibirica* which flower at the same time.

Ranunculus speciosus plenus, of gardens, is sometimes found labelled *R. gouanii*. It forms low leafy clumps of broad, buttercup-shaped leaves spotted greyish white here and there. The large flowers — some almost two inches across — form tight rosettes of closely packed petals, an acid green in the centre which gradually disappears as all become bright glistening yellow. Damp heavy soil is essential for this plant.

Ranunculus lingua is a water-loving buttercup, native to Europe and Great Britain. It is invasive so must be sited carefully, preferably in large ponds where depth of water will control it or, planted in a container, in small pools. Long spear-shaped leaves, 2 – 3 ft. tall, pierce the flat surface of the water, while branching stems carry large, yellow, buttercup flowers with shining petals. They have an impressive simplicity, while the whole plant creates a pleasing natural effect. *R. l.* 'Grandiflora' is a fine selected form with larger flowers.

Hostas

Early June finds the garden already so full of flowers that I turn for relief to the cool beauty of leaves. Nothing is more beautiful now than the expanding clumps of *Hosta* leaves. Perfectly simple in shape, often broadly heart-shaped and strongly veined in deeply indented parallel lines, the plain ones cannot be considered 'plain', a single leaf being worthy of long contemplation, while a well-established clump makes the focal point of any cool border.

By the end of May some of the variegated hostas are at their breathtaking best. *H. fortunei* 'Aurea' has delicate leaves of pale, almost lemon-peel yellow, needing to be carefully sheltered from direct sunlight which would scorch them horribly. When it first unfolds, *H. f.* 'Albo-picta' is perhaps the most spectacular of all variegated hostas. The bright primrose-yellow centre has broad margins of shaded green looking as though it has been laid on with a wet paint brush. By mid-to-end June the bright colouring of both these hostas has faded, and they become almost uniformly green.

One of the easiest and most rewarding of the variegated hostas is *H.* 'Thomas Hogg'. Throughout summer it produces a succession of fresh green pointed leaves with broad creamy-white margins. All hostas produce flowers, but the tall spires of lilac coloured trumpet-shaped flowers of *H.* 'Thomas Hogg' are among the finest.

Hosta plantaginea is much sought after for its long, white, trumpet-shaped flowers which have a delicious lily-like scent in the evening. It flowers very late in the season, sometimes too late, and is caught by frost. An excellent hybrid and offspring of *H. plantaginea* is *H.* 'Royal Standard'. It retains the same fresh green leaf colour throughout the season but makes much stronger growing plants, while beautiful heads of white flowers, sweetly scented, are freely produced.

Hostas can be found in all sizes from tiny midgets to huge ones with leaves as much as 18 inches long and 12 inches across. *H. sieboldiana* makes the largest, most sumptuous leaves, its beautiful blue-grey colouring caused by a waxen bloom.

Hostas need deep rich soil, with partial shade to protect them from burning sunlight.

Variegated and named forms are propagated by division of their densely rooted crowns. To see them in full glory they must be left undisturbed for several years and regularly fed with farmyard manure. Snails and slugs adore them and will fret them to ribbons if not destroyed.

Hosta fortunei

Papaver orientale 'Cedric Morris'

Oriental Poppies

Together with large Border Irises and perfumed shrubs of old-fashioned roses these flamboyant flowers crown an early June border. They have their faults. They take up a lot of space, some of them tend to flop, and individual flowers do not last long. But nothing else quite takes their place. I like the deeply cut foliage, heavily furred with fine silvery hairs. The huge, crumpled, silky petals can be found now in many shades, including white, ashen-pink, soft salmon, deep rose and even lilac. There is a splendid upstanding crimson called *Papaver orientale* 'Goliath' which I prefer to the orange-scarlet form which one more commonly sees; but I expect if that were rare, and the other shades were common, we should see its merits differently.

All are enhanced by a dramatic centre. A huge knob-like seed pod is covered with radiating stripes of velvet texture, dark purple in colour, surrounded by a ruff of equally dark stamens. Large, almost black blotches on the inside base of the petals stain through to the backs as pencilled veins and shadows. Nothing sets off these sumptuous flowers better than billowing clouds of grey and silver foliaged plants, with perhaps feathery columns of bronze-leafed fennel for height. Owners of meadow gardens might consider planting them among cow parsley and white marguerite daisies. All could be mowed down in late June–July with no ill effect on the poppies. I find that my grey plants usually cover up the gaps left when I cut down the finished flower stems. Gertrude Jekyll found that *Gypsophila paniculata* did the same thing very well.

Among some of the well-known forms are 'Perry's White' and 'Sultana', a lovely deep rose which does not flop. Hybridizers are constantly producing new names and forms. Among many you will find 'Black and White', a lovely pure white flower with large purple-black blotches at the base of the petals, 'Picotee' whose prettily frilled petals are salmon-red with a white base, and 'Cedric Morris', a dusty pink.

Oriental poppies will grow well in all but soggy soils, in full sun. Named varieties are grown from root cuttings. This can be done in winter, cutting the roots into pieces about 2 inches long, keeping them top side up and inserting into pots or boxes. In spring they will sprout new leaves. Old unwanted plants can be difficult to eradicate as every inch left in the soil makes a new plant.

Phlox pilosa

By the last week of June the choice for plant portraits is bewildering; all around there is scent and colour, there seems not a square foot without flowers.

I almost settled for *Gillenia trifoliata* whose flaring white petals remind me of insects' wings opening from pointed red buds and floating among wire-thin, tawny-red stems. However, a friend walking with me in the garden asked 'What is *that* pretty plant?' and my choice was made.

Phlox pilosa is one of my favourite flowering plants. I do not get on well with the large, highly-bred varieties of *Phlox*. They tend to dry out in our Essex droughts, and are martyrs to eel-worm. But this little *Phlox* never lets me down. From a running rootstock it produces masses of slender stems, about 18 inches high, set with narrow green leaves, and topped with large loose heads of cool lilac-pink flowers, sweetly scented. The flowers remain fresh throughout June, creating a low mass of delicate colour, lovely among the small butterfly blooms of *Viola cornuta*.

After the main flush, odd flower stems are produced for the rest of the summer. The wandering rootstock is no disadvantage, provided it is not placed where it would over-run tiny treasures. On the front of a herbaceous border, or in a sunny bay between shrubs would be ideal, and in any soil that does not suffer unduly from drought. In light soil I have planted it in part shade, where it flowers well and looks if anything more effective. It is lovely to pick and lasts well in water. It can be planted any time from containers (provided the soil is not bone-dry), or throughout the dormant season.

Phlox 'Chattahoochee' is another low growing phlox which is possibly a hybrid between *P. pilosa* and *P. divaricata*. I do not find it so easy to grow. Starved sand or gravel does not suit it, nor does it flourish in cold sticky clay and slugs love it. A cool, well-drained soil, laced with good garden compost suits it best, in sun or part shade. When established it is breathtaking. Placed on the edge of a border, or tumbling over a shaded ledge, its lax stems (6–9 inches long), set with small narrow leaves, carry wide loose heads of silky flowers which are an exquisite harmony of blue shades. The spaced petals are joined in the centre by a wine-red patch while the clear blue, freshly opened flowers bleach to a very pale blue as they fade, and the central zone deepens to purple.

Both these phloxes can be propagated from cuttings.

Phlox pilosa

Campanula species

Stately Campanulas

Most gardeners know the Canterbury Bell, or the Cup and Saucer Bell Flower. There are other members of the large *Campanula* family, which can add style and dignity to a mixed herbaceous border or may be used in bays between shrubs.

Campanula latifolia is a fine robust plant. Each plant produces several ramrod-stiff stems up to 4 ft. tall, set with rich green pointed leaves which get smaller as they ascend the stems. The upper half is closely set with large tubular flowers, as many as 30 to a stem, which look as though their edges have been cut, forming curled-back pointed petal tips.

Grown from seed the colours would include white and both light and dark mauvish-blue. I have a specially fine white form which has extra large flowers, over 2 inches long, of such substance that they look as handsome as Madonna lilies, but are far easier to grow. This selected form is called *C. latifolia* 'Alba'.

Campanula alliariifolia has much thinner stems which curve and bend in a most attractive way. It is ideal sprawling over the edge of a low wall or planted where it will break the hard lines of a flight of steps. Small heart-shaped leaves ascend only a short way up the stem o leave a long delicate spire of flowers. about $2\frac{1}{2}$ – 3 ft. tall. Each downcast white bell is held in a pointed calyx which is faintly stained with maroon as are the slightly furry stems. This dark colour enhances the pleated white buds which open flowers about $1\frac{1}{2}$ inches long.

Whether picked or strategically placed in the garden, I value highly these two plants for their elegant shapes. They will grow in any reasonable garden soil in full sun or part shade. They can both be grown from seed but good selected forms can be found.

On a much larger scale *C. lactiflora* is one of the most glorious sights in the late summer border. It grows wild, with other gigantic herbs, in well-watered gullies in the Caucasus. In the garden a well-established clump produces several stout leafy stems standing over 5 ft. tall. By July each stem carries a wide-branching head of blossoms so the whole plant forms a breath-taking bouquet, hundreds and thousands of open bell-flowers. Grown from seed the colours will range from pale milky-blue to a rich violet blue. You may even have a white form. All are lovely. Selected named forms can be found.

Full sun and retentive soil are required, while staking is not necessary if these plants are grouped in a site sheltered from wind, such as a bay between shrubs.

Hardy Geraniums

Sometimes called cranesbills because of their long beak-like seed pods, these plants are not to be confused with the scarlet bedding geraniums. The hardy geraniums provide the summer border or rock garden with masses of weed-smothering foliage, and an almost non-stop display of small but jewel-bright flowers.

They vary in shape and habit. Some make small compact clumps, or slowly spreading mats suited to small gardens or a raised bed. Others are wonderful fillers for large sunny borders, or cover yards of empty space between shrubs.

Geranium renardii is one of the first to flower, its pale ice-blue petals marked with fine, dark purple veins. Its leaves, arranged in neat growing clumps, are round and scalloped with a soft velvety texture, irresistible to touch.

Geranium macrorrhizum is fine for colonizing any piece of ground that does not entirely dry out in summer. It makes low-spreading carpets of strongly aromatic leaves above which stand clusters of palest pink or soft magenta flowers in June. In spring I love to see the crimson buds of *G. psilostemon* pushing through the soil to form a handsome mound of wide, deeply cut leaves. By midsummer it is a wonderful sight, crowded with magenta-crimson flowers, dramatized by black centres. Finally, the foliage develops rich autumn tints.

Some are invaluable as buffers between more dramatic, and therefore un-neighbourly, plants. Among the best is *G. pratense* which is still found wild in Britain and N. Europe. It is the old, sterile double forms which we cherish in gardens because the single forms, lovely as they are, can become a nuisance by seeding too freely.

From Kashmir comes a related form which we have long called *G. rectum album* but which is now known as 'Kashmir White'. It makes spreading clumps of finely fretted leaves above which stand 2-ft. branching stems crowded with saucer-shaped flowers, more than an inch across. They are white, finely veined with lilac.

Geranium wallichianum 'Buxton's Variety' is at its best in late autumn, unexpectedly bright and fresh among harvest scents and tones. There are many others, some in shades of purple and glowing magenta which look marvellous beneath old roses, or among silver foliaged plants.

Geraniums grow easily in most soils except those which remain soggily wet. Many will grow in full sun or part shade, while a few actually prefer shade. They range from small choice feature plants to easy and attractive ground-cover plants, ideal in large gardens.

Geranium psilostemon

Crepis incana

A Pink Dandelion

Placed on one of my sunny raised beds is a bouquet designed for a bridesmaid, made of hundreds of small pink dandelions. They are the flowers of *Crepis incana*, a plant whose leaves are shaped much like the common yellow dandelion but are grey-green in colour, felted with soft hairs, and less exuberant in growth. Instead of flowers on individual juicy stems it produces a stiff bunch of dry, thin, much branched stalks, about 12 inches tall, every one bearing neat buds which gradually open in long succession. Rows of square-tipped, pale pink petals deepen to rose towards the central point, from which spring cream-coloured stamens.

While making a plant large enough to use along the edge of a dry sunny border, it looks best perhaps on a rock garden or raised bed where it can be closely admired, and where it may be surrounded by low alpines, such as thyme mats or low carpeting sedums. I enjoy seeing the rosette-shaped flowers repeated by many different houseleeks (*Sempervivum*), some covered with silvery cobwebs, others in shades of mahogany-red or purple.

A well-drained sandy or gravelly soil, situated in full sun, is essential for this plant, which is never a nuisance distributing seedlings all over the place. In cultivation it rarely, if ever, sets seed. I increase my stock by taking root cuttings. A strong plant is dug up, preferably in spring, and several of the best, string-like roots removed. These are cut into lengths, about $1 - 1\frac{1}{2}$ inches long, and laid on the propagating table in a row, keeping the top ends all facing the same way. They are then planted upright in a shallow box, in a sandy soil mixture, the tops finally being covered with a layer of gritty sand. They are labelled, watered and watched for several weeks, keeping the box free of weed seedlings which may have appeared, until eventually new young shoots are seen, sprouting from the cut surfaces. Lift the young plants gently out of the soil, taking care not to let the newly formed roots break off. They are very brittle. Pot them individually, and shelter them in a protected place, either in a cold frame, or under a shady wall for a few weeks until they have established themselves in a new ball of soil. Then they may be confidently planted out to grow satisfactorily in their new home.

I have not yet made the dream reality, but I have long imagined this delightful plant growing in a pocket on a large terrace where it would be a joy to walk round, or sit by, in a low chair, and look down on the perfect flower arrangement.

Day Lilies

There are Day Lilies which flower in May, but most are at their best throughout July and August. As garden plants they contribute to the scene for much of the growing season. From earliest spring, when snowdrops and narcissi can look lonely against bare cold soil, they provide a background of colour and form with their vigorous clumps of newly emerging, pale green shoots. These develop throughout the summer into weed-smothering tussocks of bright green arching leaves.

There are many different species and varieties. One of the earliest is *Hemerocallis flava* whose beautiful clear yellow, lily-shaped flowers have the most exquisite fragrance, very like lily-of-the-valley. Mid-summer flowering varieties can be found in a breath-taking range of colours, including greeny-yellow, soft peach, warm apricot and glowing mahogany reds. Most of the flowers last only one day but new ones open from a cluster of buds which are held on the top of stout bare stems. They look particularly well reflected in still water, but will grow in any reasonably fertile soil, in sun, or part shade.

The petals of all *Hemerocallis* have a firm crisp texture which is why the flowers and buds have been used in salads in the far East for some thousands of years. Since learning that I have decorated my spiced rice salads with a cluster of mixed blossoms, appetizing to look at, and very exotic for a party.

Plant breeders have enjoyed themselves combining the characteristics of several original wild plants which are themselves worth seeking, such as the lovely *H. flava* whose scent has been bred into some of the yellow hybrids.

Modern varieties have larger flowers in innumerable shades on shorter stems, with less luxuriant foliage. These are good for smaller gardens, but where there is room some of the taller stemmed varieties, seen poised among fern fronds, or the sculptured leaves of *Hosta*, have greater elegance. However, I would ruthlessly chop out some of the old-fashioned varieties which carry washed-out looking flowers above heavy and depressing banks of foliage in favour of the newer varieties, with their vibrant colours, provided that the balance and pure shape of the flowers has been maintained.

Hemerocallis hybrids

Lilium martagon

Mountain Lilies

Holidaymakers scrambling in the high Alps will sometimes find with great delight a few stems of the Martagon Lily, *Lilium martagon*, tucked between boulders where grazing cows cannot reach them. It is always a thrill to see a plant which we know in our garden growing in its native habitat.

In the garden, in good soil with plenty of humus, these lilies grow much finer, standing 4–5 ft. tall with up to 50 flowers to a stem. The 'Turks'-cap' shaped flowers have thick textured petals, with a curious, not altogether pleasant scent! They vary in colour slightly, from deep maroon to light reddish-mauve, while the pale inside of the refined petals is speckled with dark maroon. The flowering season is June–July.

The lovely white form, *L. m.* 'Album', has green-shadowed, wax-white flowers, especially lovely among ferns and blue-leafed hostas in semi-shade.

I also have a variety from Dalmatia, called *L. m. dalmatica*, which has dark wine-crimson flowers on taller stems than the ordinary *L. martagon*.

Once established these lilies are long lasting and will seed themselves in favourable conditions. They thrive best in sandy loam and leaf mould but will do well in heavier soils lightened with grit and compost. You can also increase lilies by digging up a bulb, usually in August or September, and gently breaking off the scales. In a shallow box prepare a base of soil and cover this with a thin layer of sand. Gently press the base of each scale into the sand, then fill the box with sand until only the tips of the scales can be seen. The following spring, if you dig up a scale, you will see a tiny pearl-like bulb at the base. When leaves and roots appear I pot up these tiny bulbs and grow them in a sheltered frame. The next season they go into the garden, but it takes 2 or 3 more years before they make flowers.

The most fantastic of all wild lilies is *Cardiocrinum giganteum* (*Lilium giganteum*). Needing deep rich soil and regular dressings of old manure or compost, situated in a shaded, sheltered setting, it takes many years to form a bulb powerful enough to thrust up a stout hollow stem which will stand 10–12 ft. high. Shining heart-shaped leaves decorate the lower half while the towering flower spike is hung with 10-inch long trumpet-shaped, creamy-white flowers.

The bulbs which have expended this tremendous effort are exhausted and waste away, but small offsets are left behind, and will, given time and lavish feeding, repeat the unbelievable.

A Fine Spanish Grass

Certain ornamental grasses provide qualities missing in other flowering plants. Often their form and texture lightens or lifts a view which might otherwise be monotonous.

If asked to name a large and imposing grass, most people would mention Pampas Grass, *Cortaderia selloana*. Certainly it is one of the largest ornamental grasses we grow in gardens, but not everyone can provide the space it needs. Another grass, much easier to accommodate and very beautiful, is *Stipa gigantea*. For weeks in midsummer, from June till September, it enhances my garden as nothing else can.

The low-growing, dense clumps of foliage take up surprisingly little space, especially when you consider the spectacular effect of the plant in flower. Each clump will produce twenty or thirty thin, rod-like stems ranging from 4–7 ft. tall, topped with large, airy, oat-like heads. Planted against a plain background, such as the sunny side of a clipped evergreen hedge, or standing isolated among low-growing plants, it creates a unique effect; like a fountain captured in beaten gold, each flowerhead delicately made, with hundreds of pointed awns, warm honey-gold in colour held on stiff thread-like stems.

My first and unforgettable sight of *S. gigantea* was in a little paved courtyard, beside a small circular pool. The proportions of the tall shimmering vertical and still dark water were perfect.

Damp soil is not required, for this grass is found growing wild in Spain and so will stand dry conditions, flourishing in sun and well-drained soil. It can be propagated from seed, or may be divided, but only in spring.

There are several other members of this family which are worth growing, appreciated by gardeners and flower arrangers.

Stipa arundinacea (*Calamagrostis* or *Apera arundinacea*) comes from New Zealand. It makes dense clumps of fine arching leaves which become tinted bronze, red and orange in the late summer, bright as skeins of silk when caught by winter sunlight. No less lovely are the long sprays of fine, burnished-brown seed heads, as much as 3 ft. long, which tumble to the ground like a sweep of newly washed hair. Place it carefully, perhaps on a raised site or bank where the soft, strokeable tresses can be enjoyed. This grass needs a good retentive soil. It can be killed by very severe winters but provided you have allowed seeds to drop, seedlings in plenty will appear.

Stipa gigantea

Viola cornuta 'Purpurea'

Dwarf Violas

If you are accustomed to the large, kitten-faced bedding pansies (which are hybrid violas), it may take a little while to get your eye tuned to the charm of some of the dwarf violas which are little pansies, unimproved, as they are found in the wild.

One of the prettiest is *Viola cornuta* which is found in damp, sunny meadows in the Pyrenees. Its dainty flowers, about twice the size of the sweet violet, are held well above the plants on tall thin stems, creating sheets of colour in pale lavender, rich purple, and chalk white. They last for weeks in mid summer and are invaluable as an edging to semi-shady, or sunny borders provided they have enough moisture. The neat little plants creep usefully round larger plants, the flowers peering through their neighbours in friendly fashion. By the time they have spent themselves and begun to look a little untidy I shear them down, when they quickly make fresh carpets of small rounded leaves.

This invaluable little viola has hybridized with the garden pansy to produce many pretty and long-lasting violas and violettas with slightly larger flowers, and eyed and whiskered faces.

Another much admired little pansy is *V.* 'Bowles' Black', with rounded petals whose velvety blackness is lit with a tiny intense yellow eye. From early spring until winter frost it is scarcely ever without flowers, and provided it is kept to itself this enchanting little pansy sets true seed.

There are other small violas which flower only in spring. One of the best is *V. septentrionalis*. It forms hard clusters of curious jointed rhizomes which lie on the soil surface so you can see where the plants are when the leaves have disappeared in winter. In April quantities of large, pure white, violet-like flowers jostle for room among the slowly developing foliage, creating snowy-white posies along the edge of a cool shaded walk. They have no perfume. This does not detract from their beauty or value in the garden. Unlike the sweet scented violet they are not prone to attack by aphides, so for the rest of the season they give pleasure with their rich green carpets of healthy looking foliage.

All violas need humus-rich soil which does not dry out in times of drought.

Some Sea Hollies

Eryngium maritimum is our native Sea Holly, still to be found growing wild on wide and windy stretches of sand and gravel which have been swept into low dunes along unspoilt stretches of coastline. Although we grow several other relatives from foreign lands, none, I think, is more garden worthy than *E. maritimum*, if you have the conditions to suit it. In a sunny situation, in light, well-drained garden soil, it will flop its sprawly stems, handsomely clothed with leathery, prickly-edged leaves, totally unaware of drought. Strikingly blue-grey in colour they are enhanced by hard, thimble-sized cones of tiny blue flowers, surrounded by broad silver-edged spiny collars.

Eryngium alpinum, found wild in mountainous places in Europe, stands about 2½ ft. tall. Stems, branches, narrow feathery bracts, and central cones are an exquisite combination of turquoise, green and soft silvery blue. There are hybrids, including *E. × oliverianum*, which are stained much darker blue, but none has such large, or soft to touch, lace-like ruffs as does *E. alpinum*. Perhaps the prickliest of all is *E. variifolium*. Standing 18 inches tall, the leaves up the stems and the flower bracts are reduced almost to pale veins alone so that the whole stiffly branching inflorescence is a metallic silver setting for small cones of blue-shadowed flowers.

The broadest bracts are to be seen on *E. giganteum*, often called Miss Wilmott's Ghost. Wickedly prickly, silvery-green collars surround large soft-blue cones, while the whole plant fades to pale biscuit as it dries in perfect shape. This plant is a biennial, but seeds of it scattered among drought-loving plants will produce pale ghosts in scent-laden borders at dusk.

Eryngium bourgatii was introduced to gardens from the Pyrenees in 1731, but it is still not commonly grown. Yet it is one of the most beautiful. Perhaps it is because ripe seed is not always set so much further north from its native home. Where seedlings do occur they are enchanting, even as tiny plants. The individual basal leaves, outlined against dry soil, are almost round, but so deeply divided, crisply curled and prickle-edged, with broad silvered veins and scattered spots like tiny sequins, that even without flowers the plant encourages the sin of covetousness. The grey-green flowers are charmingly modest.

Most sea hollies can be grown from seed, some are propagated by root cuttings.

Eryngium maritimum

Foeniculum vulgare

Fennels

Foeniculum vulgare, Common Fennel, is sometimes seen growing wild in sandy areas along roadsides, especially in coastal districts. In dry, sunny gardens it makes a softly billowing vertical feature but you must remember to cut off the seedheads in good time to avoid a forest of seedlings. I have a large clump in the middle of my little herb garden, surrounded by low mounds of both purple and yellow-leafed sage. From early spring its newly developing stems of thread-like foliage are a pleasure to look at and delicious to taste. I like its pungent flavour of aniseed, and sometimes chop a few tender shoots to add to spring salads. I also make stuffing, together with butter and lemon peel, to put inside cleaned mackerel prepared for grilling or baking.

By mid-July established clumps of sturdy stems stand 5–6 ft. tall, forming a soft feathery column, topped with branching heads of small, yellow, cow parsley-like flowers. They make an attractive background for orange and yellow-flowered lilies growing nearby. These look well picked and arranged together in a tall jug.

The dark bronze-leafed form of fennel is especially attractive earlier in the year when the texture and colour of its young foliage makes good contrast with silver and grey-foliaged plants. When I see oriental poppies nearby, with their large, silky-petalled flowers in flamboyant shades of crimson, scarlet or rosy pinks, I am reminded of the paintings of Toulouse-Lautrec of ladies balancing cartwheel hats above feather boas.

Another dramatic fennel-like plant is *Ferula communis*. I have seen it growing wild along rocky mountain road sides in southern Europe, its great flower stems standing 10–12 ft. tall. Grown from seed, or transplanted as young pot-grown plants, it takes several years to reach maturity, when it will form a mound of leaves over 3 ft. across. These leaves are not scented, nor so finely dissected as *Foeniculum vulgare*, but the plant in flower is a wondrous sight. The leafless stems, smoothly rounded, and thick as your wrist, at first are flushed purple, fading to green, but still coated with waxy bloom. They soar high overhead carrying branching stems of yellow cow parsley-like flowers, lovely when seen against a blue sky. Full sun, well-drained soil and patience are needed to achieve this striking and unusual plant.

All fennels can be grown from seed.

Perennial Foxgloves

Apart from the well-known foxglove, *Digitalis purpurea*, and its variations, which can be obtained in white, cream and a particularly lovely peachy-pink shade, there are others which, although smaller, are a blessing because they do not die out when they have flowered. You can look forward to seeing them again another year, fulfilling their role in the pattern of plants you have arranged for them.

Throughout July I have a green-shaded walk illuminated by the pale yellow tapers of several different kinds of foxglove. *D. lutea* has the tallest, most slender spires (3–4 ft.) with very narrow flowers, closely set, on upward branching stems. The individual flowers are small but of a lovely greenish yellow, ideally suited for flower arranging. *D. grandiflora*, which used to be called *D. ambigua*, has much larger flowers, about half the size of our wild purple foxglove. The colour is soft creamy yellow with a freckled path inside the 'glove' which leads pollinating insects to the heart of the flower.

I also grow two copper-coloured foxgloves which stand well in sunnier situations. The first, which comes from meadows in the Caucasus, is *D. ferruginea*. It has 3-ft. tall, slender spires, covered with small round buds which open chubby bronze-coloured flowers. The second, called *D. parviflora*, is often scarcely recognized as a foxglove. It has short stems (about 2 ft.) closely set all round with narrow tubular flowers, greenish bronze in colour, set from tip almost to ground level. They make quiet, yet distinctive accents near the edge of a border. The seed heads of these foxgloves are attractive, both in the garden and for dried arrangements.

A hybrid foxglove, *D.* × *purpurascens*, which does not set seed, has evolved from the marriage between *D. lutea* and our own native purple foxglove, *D. purpurea*. The habit is that of *D. lutea*, forming strong basal clumps of narrow pointed leaves, smooth in texture, dark green in colour. The slender, branching flower spikes stand 4–5 ft. tall, and carry narrow tubular flowers stained pink and primrose yellow. They are very effective standing above low growing fuchsias such as *F. magellanica* 'Variegata'. It is a good perennial and can be divided in autumn or spring.

Digitalis mertonensis is another hybrid (*D. purpurea* × *D. grandiflora*) with large, crushed, strawberry-coloured flowers and soft basal leaves. It comes true from seed, and can be divided.

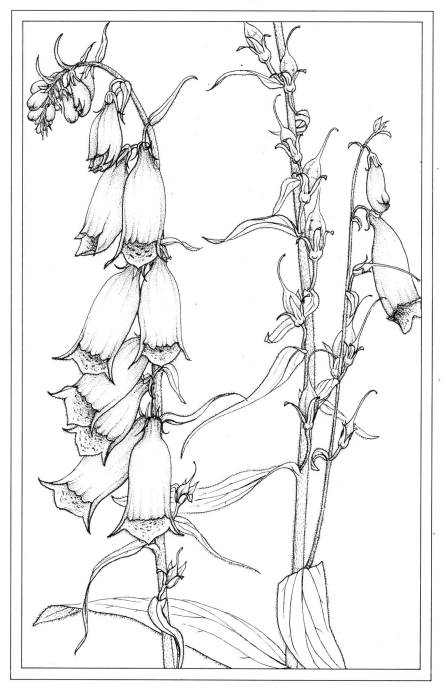

Digitalis grandiflora

Astrantia major 'Sunningdale Variegated'

The Masterworts

Although I am dazzled by the sumptuous texture and rich colour of lilies in July, I am drawn to write not about them but about a much quieter, old-fashioned looking group of plants called Masterwort, or *Astrantia*. For weeks, in mid to late summer, they provide a succession of curiously attractive flowers. Thin branching stems, about $2\frac{1}{2}$ ft. tall, carry dozens of upturned flowers, each flower resembling a tiny Victorian posy. The outer 'ruff' consists of stiff, papery petal-like bracts, while the domed centre is made up of many tiny quivering florets.

Astrantia major is usually ivory-white with pale green tips but seedlings from it may produce white flowers flushed soft pink. From the nursery of Mrs. Margery Fish came many good plants. One was an extra large form of *A. major* called 'Shaggy'. The flowers are more than twice the usual size, with many very narrow white bracts, tipped and backed with acid green. These forms, with extra large ruffs, are now recognized as a distinct botanical form, named *A. m. involucrata*.

There is also a red-flowered form called 'Rubra'. This plant has been wrongly described as *A. carniolica* which is a dwarf species. 'Rubra' is a strangely coloured flower, brilliant ruby-red in bud opening a sombre burgundy 'ruff' surrounding jade-green stamens and seed cases which eventually fill the centre. Seedlings from this plant do not all come true, but pretty rose-pink forms are worth keeping.

Astrantia major 'Sunningdale Variegated' produces some of the most vivid and beautiful variegated leaves we grow. They are at their best in spring and early summer, gradually losing their brightness as sheaves of pink-flushed flowers appear, but continuing to make a delicate display well into September.

The flowers of *A. maxima* differ in having fewer, but broader, bracts of soft rose-pink, acid green on reverse. It would be hard to pick a favourite, but *A. maxima* is one of the most desirable of all garden plants.

All masterworts are ideal for dried picture making. When pressed the little florets lie out like spokes of a wheel, making a very pretty centre rather than a squashy mess.

They need soil which does not dry out, in sun, or partial shade. They can be grown from seed, or plants can be divided in spring or autumn.

A Scabious from the Caucasus

In my early gardening days I struggled to grow the well-known *Scabiosa caucasica* 'Clive Greaves', but it did not take kindly to the sticky boulder clay of my first garden. In my present garden, in warm, free-draining gravel soil, generously fed before planting with well-rotted manure or garden compost, I have lovely beds of two other varieties which produce flowers from early summer till late autumn.

This scabious has been a popular florist's flower since it was introduced in 1803 so there are several named clones to be found, in shades of blue and white. My white form is called 'Bressingham White'. The freshly opened flowers appear almost greenish white, an impression formed possibly by the pale green bud-filled centres of fertile florets which slowly open tiny flowers filled with creamy stamens. This central posy is surrounded by an outer ring of much enlarged overlapping petals, silky and translucent in texture, finely frilled and fluted at the edges, creating a wide, flat faced flower up to 3 inches across. On long slender branching stems ($2\frac{1}{2}$–3 ft. high) they make perfect flowers for cutting which last well in water.

'Floral Queen' is the name of my blue variety. It is a soft lavender-blue, paling towards the centre which is warmed by a delicate haze of pink stamens.

These plants can be grown from seed, divisions, or cuttings in spring. They make tidy clumps of narrow, strap-shaped leaves which become deeply cut as they ascend half-way up the flowering stems. Young flowers will produce fresh flowers longer than old plants so it is advisable to divide them every few years in spring, and replant in refreshed soil.

Without wishing to confuse, I would like to introduce another grand relative of these plants which is also found in rich, moist meadows of the Caucasus. It is called *Cephalaria gigantea* (*C. tatarica* of gardens). It is not a plant for small gardens, but where there is plenty of space it is well worth considering for it introduces a flower colour which is rare in garden plants. From a stout woody rootstock (stout enough to survive naturalized in grass) comes an imposing mound of large, divided leaves. High above them are flung stiff branching stems (6–7 ft.) which carry pale, primrose-coloured scabious flowers with greenish centres. I like the way they break the skyline above surrounding plants with fresh flowers coming for weeks, on and off, until autumn. This plant can be grown from seed, or division.

Scabiosa caucasica 'Clive Greaves'

Veratrum nigrum

Veratrums

My first sight of *Veratrum album* was of isolated plants dotted about in the high pastures of the Swiss Alps. Always on north-facing slopes, often along the edges of much-trodden cattle walks where they received regular offerings of manure, were growing the finest, most elegant plants. Although not commonly seen in gardens, this plant has been cultivated since 1650. Large, broad, stiffly pleated green leaves form a basal rosette and ascend halfway up the stout stems, stopping at the base of the flowering stem. Tall heads set with short drooping side branches are closely packed with small, cup-shaped, starry flowers of palest greenish-white. The seed pods which follow dry to a soft brown shade, valued as a feature in the border as well as making an unusual profile in a dried arrangement for the house.

From America comes *V. viride* which flowers earlier and has shorter, dense heads of apple-green flowers. *V. nigrum*, the latest to flower, produces a more slender branching head of blackish-maroon flowers. All these plants need to be grown in deep moist soil, preferably in shade or part shade, to retain the perfection of the marvellously sculptured leaves, and enhance the quiet elegance of the flower spikes.

Reginald Farrer, famed for his collecting and writing of alpines, in a fit of depression surely, described them as having flowers 'of unmitigated dinginess, greenish, yellowish or grubby brownish-black'! Some observers may still agree with him. My enthusiasm for a plant may sometimes run away with my pen; the reality may not be so impressive to everyone as my description would suggest. But I think we have come to value plants much more for their foliage and form, and to see subtle beauty in quiet colours.

Veratrums can be grown from seed, but they are very slow, taking up to seven years before they flower. Underground a strong thick central root, like a parsnip, is developing, well furnished with a mass of small foraging roots. Nothing it seems can be done to hurry the stages which must be gone through before a good-sized crown will produce its first flowering stem. When well established, and well manured over many years, several crowns will have formed which will raise a plant of impressive bulk and statuesque beauty.

The Cape Hyacinths

By August the young summer freshness has gone from the garden. Many plants are already cut down. Others may be looking rather weary, affected perhaps by drought, or battered by wind. Perennial plants which emerge in truly perfect splendour during this month are worth cherishing.

Few plants in all the year can rival the elegant perfection of *Galtonia candicans*, the Cape Hyacinth, which is a bulbous plant from South Africa. Smooth stems (3–4 ft. tall) are topped with a spire of pale green buds which slowly open large, ivory-white bells. Standing in drifts behind softly rounded shapes of grey and silver-foliaged plants, with perhaps the unopened buds of *Sedum* 'Autumn Joy' providing a wax-textured, jade-green foreground, they dispel the least hint of weariness in the garden scene. They last in flower for weeks, but after that the seed heads remain as strong features, though they should be removed before they have sown their young too generously.

Galtonia princeps is a green-flowered form which opens a little earlier. It does not grow so tall, the flowers are more closely set on the stem, and are a little smaller. For many years I cultivated this bulb so indifferently that I almost decided to throw it away as a poor form. Then I relented, moved it into richer soil and was astonished at the improvement. I noticed that the foliage is much more handsome than that of *G. candicans*. The long, lax, ribbon-shaped leaves are as much as 3 inches across and are heavily coated with a waxy bloom which gives a bluish tint. The flowers improved too but are never such rounded bell-like shapes as *G. candicans*.

Lastly, *G. viride* takes the stage from August until October. It has broad, shining, rich green leaves while the large, perfectly shaped bells are palest green. They create a unique effect in the late summer border and are pounced upon by enthusiastic flower arrangers who start planning flower and fruit arrangements on sight.

These bulbs like a sunny situation in well-enriched soil. They will not produce strong stems of flower in starved conditions. They all come true from seed but take two or three years to make a flower.

Galtonia candicans

Lysimachia clethroides

Tall Relations of Creeping Jenny

Many gardeners grow Creeping Jenny, *Lysimachia nummularia*, a rapidly spreading, carpet-forming plant with prostrate stems of round green leaves and pretty cup-shaped yellow flowers. *L. n.* 'Aurea', which has lemon-yellow leaves, is not quite so well known, and might be used more often to gleam in damp, dull corners. (Its tender leaves will scorch in too bright sunlight.) More use could be made of some of Jenny's tall relatives, which thrive in sun or part shade, and make elegant spires of flower to break the monotony of more rounded shapes.

Among my favourites is *L. ephemerum*. In rich, retentive soil, in sun or part shade, it can stand over 5 ft., but 3–4 ft. is perhaps more general. Columnar, non-invasive plants are clothed with long narrow leaves set in opposing pairs. They are coated with a thin film of wax giving them a cool, grey-green appearance, very unusual and distinctive among the lush greens of the damp garden. The leaves stop at the base of the long narrowly branching heads of flower. Tiny round buds, closely set along graceful spires, open small starry white flowers over a period of several weeks. In late autumn slim wands of round brown seed pods remain to decorate the garden, and add a light touch to dried flower arrangements.

Lysimachia clethroides differs in having a running rootstock, and pointed, oval, green leaves, while its shorter, denser heads of white flowers bend over at the tip like a shepherd's crook. This plant wilts in anything but perpetually moist soil.

Another variety, wonderful for filling in large borders, perhaps between *Hemerocallis* or *Astilbe*, is *L. ciliata*. In spring the underground shoots produce a carpet of milk chocolate-brown leaves. These turn light green as the wealth of flower stems ascend, forming leafy, bushy plants about 3–4 ft. tall. From mid to late summer they are topped with wide heads of nodding lemon-yellow flowers.

Best known is *L. punctata* which is the least refined, in fact it can become a weed if planted in the wrong place, with its sturdily invasive habit of growth, but where there is room, in the wilder parts of a large garden, it stifles all opposition, and its 3 ft. stems, entirely clothed with bright yellow flowers, create bold sweeps of colour.

Polygonum amplexicaule

This handsome member of the Knotweed family comes from the Himalayas. It can form both a comfortable background and a fine feature plant in varying positions in the garden, and is alight with flower from midsummer until autumn when frost extinguishes the flaming points of colour. The slender branching stems, constantly producing new shoots, are clasped by elegant pointed leaves, which in some soils become brilliantly patterned in shades of ruby red and yellow. Generally, however, the plant forms a healthy looking bush of green foliage, about 4 ft. high and across, but it can grow taller in rich damp soil.

Polygonum amplexicaule 'Atrosanguineum' is a fine selected form bearing a long succession of slim taper-like flower spikes made up of tiny raspberry-red flowers. I also have a form with rose-pink flowers and another I treasure has spires of pure white starry flowers, enhanced with minute, dark purple stamens.

All make splendid companions for late summer and autumn flowers. In particular I think of *Aster × frikartii* 'Mönch', the best of all Michaelmas daisies, which needs no staking, is never disfigured by mildew, and provides great bouquets of large, yellow-eyed, lavender-blue daisies for weeks on end, while autumn steals about the garden.

There is a very attractive dwarf form called *P.* 'Inverleith' which stands only about 18 inches tall, with leaves and spires of flower reduced perfectly in scale. It would possibly be more welcome in a very small garden.

Another large *Polygonum* which I value very much in late summer is *P. campanulatum* (3 ft. by 3 ft.). In spring it is one of the earliest plants to clothe the ground with fresh clusters of crinkled green leaves. Throughout summer, as wide colonies of stems arise, I love to see the beautiful buff-felted backs to the leaves which are borne all along the length of the stems. Finally they are topped with loosely clustered heads of tiny rose-pink bells which, in the mass, create a frothy pink cloud, its beauty doubled when seen overhanging still water.

All these plants are easily grown in sun or part shade provided they have moderately moist soil.

Polygonum amplexicaule 'Atrosanguineum'

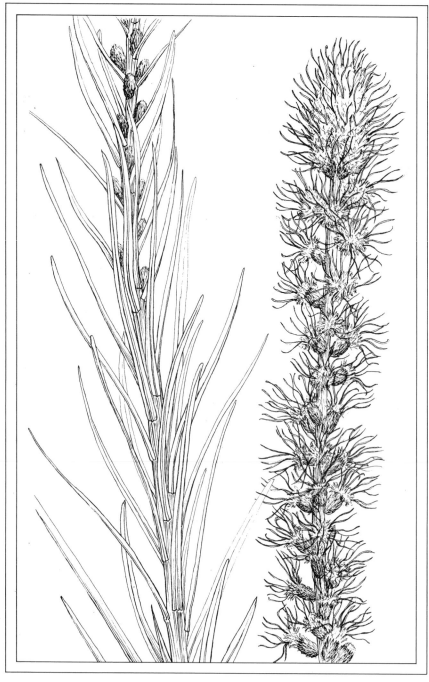

Liatris spicata

Midsummer Gayfeathers

Blazing Star or Kansas Feather, these are vivid country names which describe *Liatris*, an unusual looking family of plants, which comes from the prairies of mid-west U.S.A. They need full sun and well-drained soil, but like many meadowland plants they need plenty of humus, to ensure a fine display of flowers in August.

In shape and form they are most striking. From a basal clump of dark green, grassy leaves they send up stiffly erect stems, 2–3 ft. tall. Each stem is surrounded by fine whorls of narrow leaves which become shorter and narrower towards the top, finally petering out. Large dark buds are set against the stem, in the axils of the curving leaves, until finally at the top they form a densely packed spike. Opening from the top downwards (most plants start at the bottom and work up) the buds explode to form a foaming bottle-brush of strap-shaped petals and long curling stigmas.

Liatris spicata (18 inches–2 ft.) is one of the most vivid, with flowers of bright magenta pink. They look well rising above low mats and mounds of thyme, or set among silvery-grey foliage plants. This *Liatris* is found wild on poor dry ridges and will stand drier conditions than *L. pycnostachya* which is the Kansas Gayfeather. This, the tallest *Liatris*, will grow up to 4 ft. in good conditions.

I have a white form, *L. spicata* 'Alba' which makes larger, more fluffy heads than *L. spicata* and combines well with the blue and white flowers of *Scabiosa caucasica*.

Cutting back the flower heads of a *Liatris* immediately after it has faded can sometimes encourage the plant to flower again in late summer. They can be propagated by seed, and can also be divided in spring. They make curious clumps of root, rather like knobbly potatoes. These dense starchy crowns can be cut up with a knife and, provided each piece shows several developing shoots, they will grow away well and make good plants in the first year. They benefit from being dug up, divided, and replaced in fresh soil every 3–4 years, when they will produce much finer spikes of flower.

The Perennial Pea

Lathyrus latifolius is the name of the tumbled mass of magenta-pink pea flowers you sometimes see on railway embankments as the train hurries you by. Other people may have childhood memories of seeing it draped over a fence in a cottage garden when they were attracted by its bright colour, but disappointed by its lack of scent.

Despite that slight deficiency the Perennial Pea makes an admirable climbing plant. By August in my garden it has provided colour for several weeks. Young seed pods are already formed, but strong tendrils still carry fresh shoots and flowers high into the rich green support provided by a slim young conifer, which makes an excellent background, while nearby a variegated shrub, *Buddleia davidii* 'Harlequin', with its cream and green foliage, forms both contrast and a strong colour accent with its reddish-purple flowers.

I like even better the white flowered form called *L. l.* 'White Pearl'. Long stems of pale green buds open a close set spray of firm, perfectly shaped, ivory-white flowers, which last well when picked. I have planted 'White Pearl' where it can tangle among a low-growing, old-fashioned rose called 'De Meaux' where its beautifully formed blossoms repeat the pure white bells of *Galtonia candicans* beyond.

Plants grown from seed are not always true. To be certain that I have 'White Pearl' I take cuttings which must be rooted early in the summer to ensure that the new young plants will have developed sufficiently to make basal buds. Then new growth will emerge the following spring.

By midsummer there are dull patches in the garden which can be revitalized by these beautiful pea flowers.

I have two other scentless and perennial climbing peas. Each year, from a creeping rootstock (as have all the other peas I am describing), *L. grandiflorus*, the Everlasting Pea, makes a lighter, scrambling web of thin stems, more sparsely set with leaves, so nothing detracts from the flowers, which are in two tones of magenta-pink. They are as large as those of the scented Sweet Pea, and appear to cling like butterflies in groups of two or three to neighbouring plants or shrubs.

Lathyrus rotundifolius climbs to 5 or 6 ft. and is distinguished by its small, almost round leaves and clusters of small but eye-catching flowers in an unusual shade of coppery pink.

Lathyrus latifolius

Penstemon 'Sour Grapes'

Hardy Penstemons

From among the confusion of penstemons I have room to select only two or three favourites. With one of these I have, I fear, added to the confusion. For years I have treasured and sold a penstemon given to me by Vita Sackville-West as *Penstemon* 'Sour Grapes'; too late I have discovered that it should be called *P.* 'Stapleford Gem'. How can I correct possibly thousands of gardeners who are now treasuring my plant, wrongly labelled? I wonder does anyone possess the true 'Sour Grapes', not to be confused with another blue, 'Alice Hindley', which is not nearly so hardy, grows much taller and has larger flowers of shadowed blue.

Whatever its true name, the plant I must confess I still call 'Sour Grapes' is a treasure. To start with it is extremely hardy. I have grown it for more than 25 years without any winter protection in open borders in well-drained soil. Its flowers begin as indigo-blue buds which swell to form short, chubby flowers richly shaded with blue and amethyst while the petals flare gently into little frills. Inside the lower half of each white throat are strongly 'pencilled' purplish-red guide lines, to point the way for pollinating insects. My lasting impression of the plant is its healthy appearance with plenty of rich green shoots, the promise of flowers yet to come, while the spires of glowing blue blossoms are a feature from July to October.

Penstemon 'Garnet' also lasts well into the autumn when it is probably at its best. The narrow tubular flowers of uniform light wine or garnet-red are held on tall slender stems, lightly set with narrow leaves.

My third *Penstemon* which has survived many winters in starved gravelly soil is another hybrid called 'Evelyn'. Unlike the tender bedding type of penstemons with their large flowers and soft, easily frosted foliage, this little plant has slimmed everything down so that its chances of survival are much improved. Standing only about 18 inches tall, it makes compact little bushy plants set with very narrow leaves, topped throughout summer with dainty spires of narrow, palest pink flowers, the colour deepening at the fluted edges of the petals.

In very cold districts it would be wise to place all these penstemons under the shelter of a warm wall. They usually sprout again from the woody base if the top growth is badly damaged. They strike easily from cuttings, taken in late summer, and sheltered from severe winter weather as insurance for the following spring.

Japanese Anemones

In both form and colour these are among the most beautiful of garden plants. Their soft pink or white flowers seem still part of summer, though the early morning garden is draped with dew filled cobwebs, and there is a smell of decay in the air. But everything about these plants is fresh and elegant.

The varieties we see cultivated are called *Anemone × hybrida*, being hybrids between several wild species. Some are single, some semi-double, some will grow up to 5 ft. if planted in favourable conditions. Others may be shorter, and some can be placed near the edge of the border. One of my favourites is the old-fashioned 'Honorine Jobert' which in well-fed retentive soil will grow 4–5 ft. high, producing many stately branching stems which carry a long succession of pure white, shallow-cupped flowers, their centres held together by bright green knobs around each of which radiates a ring of quivering orange stamens. The other well-known form, the common pink Japanese Anemone, has the palest pink petals inside while the dark rose shadows on the reverse side deepen the tone as sunlight shines through them.

Another lower growing Japanese Anemone has a double layer of much narrower rose-coloured petals which are almost quilled as they become pinched together at the centre. This could be a hybrid of *A. hupehensis* called 'Prince Henry'.

All are set off by basal clumps of firm, dark green leaves, each divided into 3 parts. The only disadvantage to these lovely plants is that when well suited they do increase by means of colonizing roots, but provided they are wisely sited this is to be welcomed. They do best in retentive soil, even stiff heavy soils including those based on lime or chalk. In such conditions they make imposing groups provided they have been given a good start with the addition of well-rotted humus. They look good against a background of shrubs with perhaps a fine grass like the tall *Miscanthus sinensis* 'Gracillimus' to complement them.

Named forms are easily propagated by detaching some of the horizontal wandering roots which bear small white, pointed buds. If these are cut into small lengths and potted in October–November, they will make strong young plants by the following autumn.

Anemone japonica × hybrida

Ligularia dentata

Gigantic Groundsels

If you possess a piece of perpetually soggy soil then you might treat yourself to one or two members of the *Ligularia* family. They are some of the most spectacular plants we can grow, astonishing relations of that familiar little nuisance, Common Groundsel, *Senecio vulgaris*.

Ligularia dentata 'Desdemona', once known as *Senecio clivorum*, is never dull from the moment its first leaves appear in spring. Round in shape, at first they are marvellously shiny with a rich red-mahogany colour flushing both sides. At this stage you should hurry to put down bait to protect them from voracious slugs and snails. By August the leaves have become much larger, sometimes more than a foot across, with strong purplish-red veins puckering the dark matt-green surface while the rich beetroot-purple tint of the undersides is emphasized by the spokes of shining veins. Thick, purplish-red flower stems emerge above the handsome pile of leaves carrying heads of large orange daisies with brown-ringed centres. Honey bees and bumble bees stagger around the pollen-filled centres, while I stand, waist deep, among these fiery flowers dazed by the rich glow of colour.

Although they grow well in full sun if planted in really wet soil, a sudden heatwave will cause the great leaves to wilt temporarily. They will tolerate slightly less moist soil in situations where they cannot be scorched by strong sunlight.

For those who may find this combination of size and colour rather too much there is a *Ligularia* which is more restrained in colour yet still noble in effect. *L.* 'Gregynog Gold' is a superb hybrid raised in Wales (hence the spelling!). Large rounded, but cool green leaves make imposing groups provided you do not forget to keep up the attack against slimy greedy feeders. Fretted with holes all these plants can be a dismal sight, but in late summer there is nothing more spectacular that the fine conical heads composed of large, clear yellow daisies which stand well above the mounds of lush leaves.

There are several other garden-worthy members of this family, including some with much smaller yellow flowers held in slender spires standing up to 6ft. tall. Perhaps the best is *L.* 'The Rocket' which flowers earlier, in July, but whose dark stemmed seed heads still provide an interesting background. Ligularias can be grown from seed, or division of named varieties.

Calamintha nepetoides

In the middle of a sunny yard outside my back door I have a small herb garden, handy to the kitchen. Among thyme and sage bushes I have planted *Calamintha nepetoides* which is not a cooking herb, but creates a busy atmosphere, humming and buzzing with bees. At first sight it is not at all an impressive plant. During the early part of the summer it makes modest bushy plants covered with small, dark green leaves which have a powerful aromatic scent. By August stiff spires of tiny, pale blue flowers, like ghosts of the summer-flowering catmint, begin to open, too small to attract attention at first, but as the weeks go by you are drawn to the ever-increasing haze of pale blue, while honey bees stumble ecstatically in and out of every tiny blossom.

It is the kind of plant where one looks lonely, two or three look better and a crowd looks best, especially if you have room to group them on the edge of a sunny border. Provided no severe frost occurs, these little bushlets continue to produce fresh spires of blue-lipped flowers until the end of November. Even then, when the scarlet and gold leaves of a Chinese vine are sent rustling round my little courtyard, in the chill of late afternoons I am cheered to stoop and pick a few fresh flower spikes together with a cluster of the grey-purple leaves of purple sage (*Salvia officinalis* 'Purpurascens') which grows nearby, and then complete a little bunch for my writing table with a handful of a tiny branching daisy called *Erigeron mucronatus*. All these simple plants look well growing together and make a picture for months on end.

Cuttings of *Calamintha* root easily in June when they will have time to make sturdy plants before the winter. They will grow in any well-drained fertile soil. Surviving the tidying-up of the local road sweepers along the roadside verge a few yards from my garden entrance there grows a rather battered specimen of our native *C. officinalis*, which is a little smaller in habit, but very similar. *C. nepetoides* is found wild on rocky debris in the mountains of southern Europe. It can also be grown from seed.

Calamintha grandiflora is a close relative, and another modest plant which has won my admiration by sheer persistence and durability. It makes low-growing, clumpy plants, dressed in pale green aromatic leaves and small, pink, sage-like flowers. At first I thought these little flowers looked spotty, but the plants keep up such a display throughout the summer, both of fresh foliage and flower, that I have come to value them tucked in among more flamboyant neighbours. This *Calamintha* can easily be pulled apart in spring. It also seeds itself.

Calamintha nepetoides

Kirengeshoma palmata

Kirengeshoma palmata

There is no plant in the garden to compare with this cool oriental beauty which keeps us waiting almost until the end of the flowering season before we can stand and wonder at its strange perfection. *Kirengeshoma palmata* is found growing wild in woodland on some of the Japanese islands, but even there it is rare.

In the garden it dies away completely in winter, but each spring, from a deep rootstock, come many tall (4 ft.) smooth stems, stained purplish-maroon on their upper side where the light falls on them. Throughout the summer they carry handsome leaves shaped rather like those of a plane tree, with slightly serrated edges. Towards the top of the stems, the leaves, set in pairs, become much smaller, and from the axils of the leaf stalks are produced the flowering stems. The flowers begin to open about the end of August until the end of September, even later in cooler districts. Heavy sprays of fat, swelling buds are held in such prominent, cupped calyces they remind me of hazelnuts, while the weight of them causes many of the slender stems to arch until the flowers almost touch the ground. Slowly the buds lengthen and extend lemon-peel yellow petals into shuttlecock-shaped flowers, about $1\frac{1}{2}$ inches long. They are curiously thick in texture, and as they fade the colour becomes pale butter-yellow.

Tidy gardeners tend to rush in with canes and other paraphernalia to tie up these wayward beauties, but I love to see them bowed in deep obeisance, in shadowed recesses, among ferns and woodland grasses.

To be confident that you will see this plant growing to perfection great care must be taken in choosing and preparing its site. Semi-shade and shelter from damaging winds are essential. So too is a lime-free, deeply moisture-retentive soil, well enriched with humus.

My plants do not seed very freely but some flowers which have become fertilized gradually form a large, swollen pod within the cup-shaped calyx, once again looking very like a large filbert nut except for three long pointed horns (really the remains of the stigmata) which protrude like antennae, or spider's legs. To the end this plant is unusual.

Black-eyed Susan

The proper name for Black-eyed Susan is *Rudbeckia fulgida*, and this name belongs to the plant found growing wild in damp sunny meadows in North America. In the garden we grow several named forms which have been selected as being especially fine.

Rudbeckia fulgida 'Goldsturm' makes healthy looking clumps of dark green, smooth-textured leaves above which stand compact branching stems (2–2½ ft.) carrying from midsummer onwards a long succession of bright yellow daisies. They are distinguished by their almost black, hard, cone-like centres, and somewhat drooping broad petals. Provided we have no frost this splendid plant, if grown in rich retentive soil, will still be full of fresh flower in November.

Rudbeckia fulgida 'Deamii' opens its first flowers a little later, on slightly taller stems (2½–3 ft.). Another difference is that its leaves are quite bristly to touch.

Rudbeckia nitida is a very tall-growing cone-flower. Standing easily 7 ft. high it does tend to be blown about if not supported, but I love its clean fresh look in late summer. Rich dark green foliage is set off by the display of large, clear yellow daisies which have pale green, central cones. There is a double version of this called 'Goldquelle', of which I am not so fond.

Echinacea purpurea, which used to be called *R. purpurea*, is a close relative of the cone-flowers. It makes strong stately plants well furnished with good foliage and large, handsome daisy flowers. The wide-rayed petals are a strange dusky crimson-red which makes an amazing contrast to the glistening burnt-orange centre. This is constructed like a cone-shaped brush with short firm bristles set in spiral formation. In fact these 'bristles' are individual fertile flowers which erupt with bright orange dots of pollen.

Good selected forms include 'Abendsonne' which has petals of a lighter, less purple shade of pink, while 'Robert Bloom' is a splendid richly coloured form. It starts quickly opening its first flowers in July but as it continues over the next two to three months to produce more and more on side branches it gradually builds up a stunning display. 'White Lustre' is a white-flowered cultivar from America.

Unlike rudbeckias, which are not fussy about soil so long as it does not dry out, the echinaceas do best in richly fed, well-drained soil.

Rudbeckia fulgida

Clematis flammula

Small Late Flowering Clematises

If you know only clematises with flowers the size of tea plates, and names like 'Nelly Moser' or 'The President' then you might be forgiven for failing to recognize some of the tiny-flowered relatives as being members of the same genus. Many a visitor has eyed me with grave doubt when I have been trying to convince them that a plant I have in the garden really is *Clematis heracleifolia davidiana* 'Wyevale'. Repetition of the absurdly long name does nothing to help. This very unusual clematis produces from a woody base several stiff stems (3–4 ft. tall) carrying large handsome leaves. In late summer clusters of buds appear in the cradles formed by the leaf stalks, slowly opening small, sweet scented, almost stemless flowers, shaped very much like individual hyacinth flowers, soft powder blue in colour.

If I remind you that Old Man's Beard, often seen festooning blackberry hedges, is *C. vitalba*, then it may help to visualize the effect of other small flowered clematises. *C. × jouiniana* makes a wild tangle of long scrambling stems which look equally well sprawling down a bank, or trained over a dead tree stump. Throughout August and September its rich green foliage is smothered beneath a froth of small blue and white flowers.

Clematis flammula I almost threw out as a young plant, bearing as it did but a few wispy trusses of creamy white star-shaped flowers, but now that it spreads a great fan of shoots up one side of a wall, dropping half way down the other side, and forms a foaming mass of curiously scented blossom (some say like almonds) from mid-August to the end of September, I have changed my mind, and consider it to be one of the best of late flowering clematises.

Clematis rehderiana is among the last to flower. All summer it busies itself making a scrambling bower of long trailing shoots, covered with small divided leaflets which are very downy, especially when young. By September panicles of small bell-shaped flowers appear in the leaf axils throughout the entire length of the long trailing stems, which may be covering a large shrub or trailing for yards across the ground. The colour is that pale greenish-yellow which one remembers as primrose-yellow, and if you smell them you will be reminded of cowslips.

Dwarf Astilbes

Most people would love to grow astilbes, they are such attractive plants, but unless some moisture remains in the soil throughout the summer we should not really be tempted to try them. However, being gardeners, we are often tempted to grow something in less than ideal conditions and, despite their delicate almost fragile appearance, astilbes are tough hardy plants. They prefer moist, even boggy soil, and will thrive in full sun provided they never go short of water. However, drier soils can be made acceptable if the site is in partial shade, preferably not infested with hungry tree roots, and if every effort is made to improve the soil with moisture-retaining material.

Dwarf astilbes are perhaps the easiest to grow, ideally placed along the edge of a cool border, or tucked into a damp pocket in the rock garden. A good mulch of either peat or pulverized bark helps to retain moisture and suppress weeds, but once the plants are established their attractive foliage makes very satisfactory ground-cover.

Astilbe 'Sprite' is charming in every way, beginning with its neat clusters of finely cut, shining, dark green leaves. They set off admirably the wide, feathery sprays of shell-pink flowers held on thin, wiry stems about 12 inches high. Long after the flowers have faded the bright, rust-coloured seed heads continue to add warm hues to the autumn scene.

Astilbe 'Bronze Elegance' differs in having less finely cut leaves which are attractive in spring being pale green, slightly tinted reddish-bronze. This has almost totally faded by the time the flowers appear, which differ from *A*. 'Sprite'. They are not so feathery but create a very pretty two-tone effect as the tiny flower buds open creamy-peach, deepening to soft rose-pink as they mature.

Last to flower, and continuing to make a display for weeks into September is *A. chinensis* 'Pumila'. Dense, creeping carpets of matt green leaves make good ground-cover by the damp edges of a pool, or alongside a cool shaded border. I love the stiffly upright, almost taper-like flower spikes, with very short side branches, closely set with luminous flowers made of rose-pink clusters almost buried beneath lilac-mauve fluff. By autumn these remain, dense yet slender spires, in soft buff shades, standing about 15 inches tall.

All astilbes are easily increased by division.

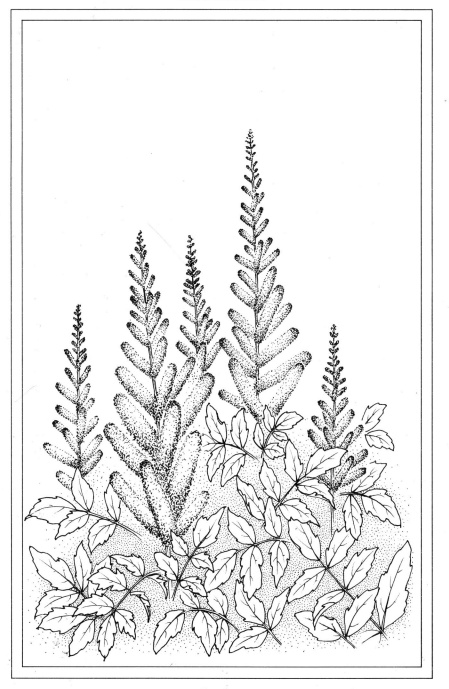

Astilbe chinensis

Zauschneria californica

The Hummingbird Trumpet Flower

With my poor gravel soil almost bone-dry after several weeks of drought, I have special affection for any plant which manages to retain its foliage and produce, for weeks on end, a brilliant display of flower. *Zauschneria californica* is such a treasure. I have a form called *Z. c.* 'Dublin' (syn. 'Glasnevin'). In winter it disappears, and after a specially severe winter I hover over the empty space, wondering if it will ever reappear. But the advantage of poor stony soil is that it is warm in winter. It cannot hold cold or frozen water, so the wandering underground shoots emerge full of life in spring. By September they have made a little colony of thin dry wiry stems, almost 2 ft. high. They are reddish-brown in colour, set with tiny, narrow green leaves and carry erect long sprays of brilliant orange-scarlet flowers. Each flower is over an inch long, a slender narrow tube ending in a widely flaring trumpet from which protrude, still further, the long-stemmed anthers and pistil, which are also scarlet. In its native home, in central and southern California, hummingbirds hover among the flowers searching with their long bills for the nectar which lies at the base of each long tube. Hummingbirds are attracted to scarlet flowers; bees cannot see them.

I have another form called *Z. cana* (*Z. californica microphylla*) which has much narrower leaves. In a very hot, sunny situation the tangle of slender woody stems, narrowly set with side branches, becomes pale ashen grey as the leaves intensify their protection against evaporation. This colour is more effective than green leaves, providing a brilliant contrast for the scarlet flowers, but unfortunately the flowers do not continue over such a long period. The flowers of *Z. c.* 'Dublin' still make a show in my garden in November, eclipsed only by the radiant pile of hardy *Agapanthus* leaves nearby, which die in glowing shades of honey, gold and amber.

Much as we may enjoy the late September heat and sunshine, it is often a trying time for plants, when they have to struggle against this final period of drought, so often a feature of our East Anglian climate. In such conditions, on each dry day, I am enchanted by those little tongues of fire which flicker among my grey and silver plants. In very cold districts with heavy wet soils these plants would not be long lived.

Colchicums

Dewy September mornings encourage the colchicums to show off beautiful, large, crocus-like flowers which emerge straight from the bare soil without leaves. Rich lilac-rose in colour, poised on slender white stems they are known by some as 'Naked Ladies' (because of their lack of leaves) but more generally as 'Autumn Crocuses'. In fact they are not crocuses at all, but belong to the lily family.

In mid-winter their tightly rolled clusters of leaves are already starting to push through the bare soil, a welcome sight when the days are dark and the nights too long. By March and April, when the garden can still be uncomfortably chilly and bare I love to see the bold clusters of broad and shining rich green leaves, larger and more prosperous looking than almost anything else at that time of year. They make good use of every gleam of sunlight, and the slowly warming moisture in the soil, to feed large corms deep below. By June, their work done, they collapse and die, their withered, ragged remains being a source of discontent to tidy-minded gardeners. In some situations they would be unsightly, but in most gardens a spot can be found where this 'untidiness' could be overlooked for the sake of the glorious display of even one clump of gorgeous blossoms. No other corm or bulb is so generous, with more than twenty buds and flowers pushing up from an established clump.

Once you have discovered them you will find there are many varieties and forms. In colour they range from palest cyclamen-pink to rich ruby shades. Some are heavily chequered with dark centres, others have startlingly white throats. In some the petals are narrow and open flat and starlike, while there are to be found double forms which are extraordinary and beautiful. None can compare with *Colchicum speciosum* and its forms which have the largest, perfectly rounded, goblet-shaped flowers. Most breath-taking of all is the white *C. s.* 'Album' which flowers into October. So late in the year, pure in shape and colour as the snowdrops to come, these marble white chalices fill you with wonder as they stand alone among the decay of autumn.

In large gardens vivid drifts of colour can be swirled around the edge of shrubberies, or scattered about in a bulb lawn provided you remember to cut the grass close just before the flower buds emerge. Colchicums flourish in any soil provided they are not starved, and can be grown in sun or part shade. Single corms take several years to make a clump of corms, seed takes five years or more to make a flowering plant.

Colchicum autumnale

Phytolacca clavigera

Poke Weed

Phytolacca, also known as Poke Weed, or Red Ink Plant, is a large coarse-growing plant which never fails to draw attention in the right setting. It could not be called a pretty plant, while its black evil-looking berries, full of purple staining juice, are poisonous, but it has great character, not overlooked by either good gardeners or flower arrangers who recognize its value.

There are two kinds: one is *P. clavigera* from Yunnan, in S.W. China. A large woody rootstock produces fresh each year stout branching stems which can make a framework 4 ft. high and as much across. Set with large oval leaves up to 6 inches long the foliage alone is valuable in contrast to smaller leafed shrubs. In June every branching stem holds an upturned, densely set spike of small shocking-pink flowers, each with a small green eye. These gradually become spikes of small green berries until, in September, they are purple-black, while the stems which support them have become vivid carmine-red. When the berries have vanished into the crops of immune birds there is still shape and colour left behind in the spire of 'flowers' formed by tiny maroon bracts.

Phytolacca americana is similar in size and habit, but it flowers a little later. The flowers are white and the berries do not become so completely round as those of *P. clavigera*, but retain a shape like a peeled tangerine, each shining black, juicy segment containing a seed.

There may be readers who question the wisdom of growing poisonous plants in the garden. Certainly children should be warned: in my experience they take such advice very seriously. But we should deprive ourselves of many favourites—columbines, hellebores, lilies-of-the-valley and foxgloves to name but a few—if we aimed to grow only those which are harmless. As gardeners we learn to live with, and respect, many plants. Simply washing our hands before eating is all that is needed in most cases for protection.

Some people are allergic to the touch of plants: itching, rashes or blisters may be caused. Thin rubber gloves are the answer to this, and learning to keep ones arms and legs protected.

The phytolaccas require retentive soil, and will grow in sun or shade.

Nerines

Nerines are bulbous plants found wild in South Africa. They provide some of the most exotic-looking flowers we can grow in late autumn. Seen at this time of the year in florists' displays they look as if they must surely have been grown in a greenhouse, but planted in spring, in the shelter of a warm sunny wall out of doors, they flower generously.

Nerine bowdenii is most usually grown, and once established a tight clump of bulbs will be formed, sending up a succession of flowers from late September to early November. Smooth green stems (18 inches – 2 ft.) carry a cluster of lily-shaped flowers. Each flower has six slightly frilled petals, each turned back to form a curled tip. The colour, light rose-pink, is riveting when seen in a setting of 'autumn mists and mellow fruitfulness'. The glistening texture reminds me of sugar icing, as do the pale and deep tones in each flower, as though the colour were not mixed too carefully. Pale, long-stemmed anthers flare forward, tipped with purple pollen sacs.

Nerine bowdenii 'Fenwick's Variety' has larger but paler flowers, while *N. undulata* has spidery flowers of more delicate texture. The closely packed bulbs like to jostle near to the surface, half exposed, so they may be baked by the summer's sun. When you plant them in a well-drained, sunny position you should leave their tops just showing, so it is wise to cover them with a good mulch before really bitter frosts are expected which would destroy them; but remember to remove it in spring.

Much less commonly seen are the white forms of *Nerine*. *N. bowdenii* 'Alba' is not truthfully pure white. Its large frilled petals are just faintly washed with pink, but the flowers of *N. flexuosa* 'Alba' have not the slightest hint of pink. They are white shadowed with green when first they open, but to pay for this purity we have to accept rather smaller flowers. Both these forms have survived outside in my well-drained gravel soil, well mulched with small grit in winter.

Nerine sarniensis has survived several winters but not flowered outside; it does flower, however, in my cool greenhouse. Grown in pots the flowers are breathtaking, being bright sealing-wax red, dusted with glistening gold.

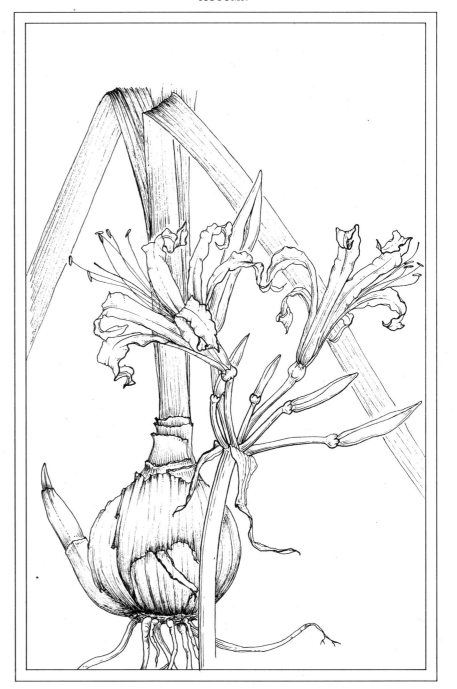

Nerine bowdenii

Crocus speciosus

True Autumn Crocuses

Some people may be surprised to learn that there are true crocuses which naturally flower in autumn. What a delight they are, suddenly appearing through the warm moist soil, their translucent petals glowing with fresh, vivid colour. They are more refined than the solid Dutch cultivars of spring, which have their merits so I would not wish to slight them, but the wild crocuses increase more quickly into drifts and scatterings of cool lilac and blue, wonderful contrast for the flaming colours of autumn.

Crocus speciosus appears first. Slim indigo buds on dark stems pierce the soil without leaves. Warmed by the sun they open wide-cupped blue petals feathered with purplish-blue veins. The white form always appears late while you wait in despair lest some evil pest has destroyed it.

Crocus sativus is another, most handsome. Its light purplish petals are striped with deeper purple veins which merge into a dark shadowed throat out of which spill three long scarlet ribbons. Rub them between your fingers and you will see the strange yellow stain which was used to colour sticks of barley sugar, and which today we use to make saffron rice. Commonly called the Saffron Crocus it was once grown in Britain as a crop, Saffron Walden presumably being a centre of production, but today it is not free flowering enough to be a commercial proposition; just imagine bending your back long enough to pick a pound of those scarlet threads!

There are many more true autumn crocuses found wild in high mountain pastures or rocky hillsides in the warm countries around the Mediterranean.

I like to see them suddenly appear in September among my grey and silver borders where the southern scented plants are usually looking very well, being then less troubled by desiccating heat and drought, and having been induced to make new growth by a light trim in July. However, there is not much colour at that time of year so a scattering of these fresh little flowers is most welcome around the edges of cistus bushes or santolinas. I try to keep them out of my best thyme mats where their clumps of grassy leaves in spring can leave unsightly ragged holes. Crocuses, both spring and autumn flowering, look best perhaps in fine, close cut grass. But it takes time and experience to retain only the fine grasses, and of course you must have a site where bulb leaves can be allowed to wither naturally in long grass before being mown, usually towards the end of June depending on how many different bulbs you grow.

Crocuses grow easily in most soils and situations excluding ill-drained soil or deep shade.

Propagation is by seed, although many do increase vegetatively.

Hardy Lobelias

When meeting these tall dramatic plants for the first time it is not surprising that some people fail to see any relationship with the low-growing, blue-flowered bedding *Lobelia*. But if you look closely you will see the flower shape is the same, with a broad upper petal partially divided into three while the lower two petals are reduced to ribbon-like strips.

Among the varieties we grow in gardens are some hybrids between two American plants. *Lobelia cardinalis* is found in marshy meadows, throughout the eastern United States and Canada. It has scarlet flowers and green leaves. *L. fulgens*, from marshy places in Mexico, is very similar but has reddish stems and leaves. It is not, however, so hardy. A marriage between these two has produced plants with deep beetroot-coloured leaves and stems ($2\frac{1}{2}$–3 ft. tall), and large spires of intensely scarlet flowers. 'Queen Victoria' and 'Bees' Flame' are two of these well-known hybrids. Another form I have is called 'Dark Crusader' with greyish-green leaves stained with purple and flowers of glowing blood-red.

Not all are reliably hardy. A good mulch of peat, or leaf-litter is enough to protect the new buds which are just beneath the soil surface. They can be tempted to emerge too soon in our mild winters, to be killed by spring frosts.

To increase selected and named forms these plants must be propagated vegetatively. In March old clumps can easily be divided into individual rosettes. A more exciting way is to make leaf cuttings. In July select a strong stem and remove the upper spire of flowers. Cut the stem into pieces about one inch long. Each piece will bear one leaf. Insert the prepared stems into a shallow tray filled with a rooting compost and stand in a covered propagating tray, or under mist. In a few weeks roots and a new basal shoot will appear, but keep these young plants well protected until the following spring when they may be hardened off and eventually planted out.

Lobelia × *vedrariensis* is a more reliable hybrid with long lasting spires of rich violet-purple flowers, valued in the autumn as contrast to the many daisy-shaped flowers.

Lobelia syphillitica produces 2–3 ft. spires of smaller flowers, of a remarkable clear shade of blue, lasting many weeks as a fine feature. However, the plants tend to deteriorate if left undisturbed. They need to be divided in spring and replaced in fresh soil every few years.

All these late summer flowers will grow in full sun, but need moisture retentive soil.

Lobelia × *vedrariensis* and *L.* 'Queen Victoria'

Liriope muscari

Liriope muscari

This is a strange but intriguing plant found wild along the edges of woods in Japan and China. In gardens it will grow almost anywhere provided the soil is reasonably fertile and not too dry. I like the dense, arching tufts of narrow, glossy, dark green leaves which are a feature in winter as well as in summer. Split up and replanted in groups in spring they make useful ground-cover. They also provide a contrast of texture and form among soft, rounded leaves.

For those whose first question is always 'What kind of flower does it have?', I suppose I could say it is a bit like the spring *Muscari*, the Grape Hyacinth. Standing 12–15 inches tall the straight stems are tinted dark purple while the top half forms a narrow spire clustered with small, upturned flower buds, pale violet in colour, firmly and secretively closed. When I first saw them they called to mind those hideously sprayed branches one used to see in shops spattered with some drops of plastic material intended for winter decorations. But now with more devoted observation, and understanding of where and how to plant them, their texture and shape remind me of little seed pearls. Their delicate colour tends to be bleached in strong sunlight; I have better stems of flowers where they are partially shaded. There is a white form which I have been sent by kind readers on learning that I had not seen it. I also have a little of the variegated form, with leaves almost totally cream, but it suffers from delicate health, so propagation is very slow indeed.

An even more curious relative of *Liriope* is *Ophiopogon planiscapus nigrescens*. It makes much the same shaped arching clumps of narrow, strap-shaped leaves, but their colour never fails to produce a shower of comment, not always complimentary. It is black — even checking in winter I have surprised myself by holding a leaf against a black painted hinge and seeing no difference! In summer you will find short stems of little lilac-coloured, bell-shaped flowers tucked among the leaves, while elongated sprays of shining purple-black berries remain long into winter. This plant increases by underground stolons and, like *Liriope*, looks well in winter. I am however still experimenting to find the right companions to set off its strangely provocative character.

A Grass Family from Japan

Even enthusiastic gardeners tend to wince at the word 'grass'. It either suggests that the lawn needs mowing, or some bed is greened over with annual meadow grass. Ornamental grasses are still not readily considered as garden plants, which is a pity, because they make a change of texture and form which is often lacking in otherwise good pieces of planting. Part of the trouble is, I suspect, that most people are looking for colour in flowers, not recognizing that good shapes can create a scene for a much longer period.

The *Miscanthus* family, a tribe of tall-growing, spectacular grasses, look especially well in autumn. Although they make slowly increasing root stocks they are not invasive. In reasonable soil, in full sun or part shade, they send up clumps of strong stems over 6 ft. tall, each clothed from top to bottom with long, cascading, ribbon-like leaves which flutter in the breeze and create an elegant columnar shape when still. By the end of October the pinky-beige flower heads appear, held upright like closed shuttlecocks on damp days, opening into fluffy, feather dust-mops when dry. *M. sinensis* 'Silver Feather' flowers freely. *M. s.* 'Gracillimus' rarely flowers. Its much narrower leaves have a conspicuous silver central vein all summer until autumn frosts bleach the shimmering column to palest straw colour.

Miscanthus sinensis 'Variegatus' makes a dramatic feature plant throughout the growing season with leaves conspicuously striped with white along their whole length. *M. s.* 'Zebrinus' on the other hand sometimes alarms new owners who promptly think they have bought the wrong plant as its rich green leaves show not a sign of any variegation until late July when bands of yellow appear across the leaves. This, together with the soft graceful form and silky, pinky-brown flower heads, regularly produced in autumn, makes this a most desirable grass.

All miscanthuses make good backgrounds, even windbreaks for late summer and autumnal flowering plants. But planted singly, as a feature beside water, or on the edge of a piece of paving, every line they produce will make part of the picture.

They are easy to grow in all but drought-stricken soils, and should be divided and replanted in spring, never in autumn.

—89—

Miscanthus sinensis 'Zebrinus'

Tricyrtis formosana

The Toad Lilies

Anyone who sees *Tricyrtis formosana* for the first time is drawn by its quaint beauty. A member of the Lily family, nicknamed Toad Lily because of its spotted flowers, it is not large flowered nor does it make bulbs, but has an underground root system which throws up a crowd of stems standing 2–3 ft. high. Each purplish-tinted stem carries ranks of shining dark green leaves, oval shaped and deeply veined. At the top of each is a branching head set with clusters of purple-stained buds. These open over many weeks in autumn to show small lily-shaped upturned flowers. Looking closer you will see that each waxen flower is really white inside, but so heavily spotted it appears purple. The intriguing and indescribable centre, and both the back view and profile of these small flowers (scarcely an inch across), combine to produce a plant that has more than a little charm, whether you see it floating upwards to face you in the garden, or examine each flower minutely from the comfort of your armchair. They are plants to contemplate, not to use as eye-catching colour from yards away.

There are other kinds. *T. hirta* has matt, slightly hairy leaves, with flowers carried more densely on narrower spires. They are a little larger, and pale lilac in colour. I also have a white form, *T. h.* 'Alba'. Its green-washed buds open to show white, wax-like flowers with the important central stigma and stamens in cream. This plant needs a warm sunny site to encourage the flowers which open late in the season.

Tricyrtis macropoda is the first to flower, in August, with pale, creamy-yellow flowers, finely peppered with maroon. These dots become fewer and larger towards the heart of the flower.

The other tricyrtises flower from September until November provided they have good moisture-retaining soil to keep their foliage through possible summer droughts. Use plenty of well-rotted compost when planting. They will grow in part sun or shady conditions, but not too dark as they need the ebbing power of late autumn sunshine. They look well among hostas, with a few colchicums in the foreground to intensify the colour scheme. They are long-lasting perennials, requiring no support, and can be planted throughout the dormant season, although container grown plants can be moved almost anytime.

Geranium 'Buxton's Variety'

The hardy *Geranium wallichianum* was originally found in the Himalayas growing in damp valley meadows and along wood edges. This form is a treasure among many other good cranesbills, and since it saves its main display for late summer and autumn it needs and deserves a good retentive soil. The best-known form is *G. w.* 'Buxton's Variety', selected by E. C. Buxton at Betws-y-coed, North Wales. Starting quietly in midsummer the ever-lengthening stems carry a non-stop display of flowers which are at their best in September and October, with a scattering of fresh flowers continuing until frost in November finally withers them.

There are infinite shades and tones of blue in the garden, but some are breath-catching, and this is one of them. Each perfect, saucer-shaped flower consists of five rounded petals of which only the outer edge is broadly banded with blue, and this blue is not really pure for, from it dissolve pencil-thin red veins which radiate across the startling white central zone to be joined in the centre with a cluster of dark dots, the purple-black anthers.

The habit of the plant is pleasing. Lax, coral-tinted stems radiate from a central point to sprawl along the ground, or even climb into accommodating neighbours. The pink-tinged leaves of *Ajuga reptans* 'Burgundy Glow' and the dark purple leaves of *Viola labradorica* provide a rich colour contrast on the ground, while hardy fuchsias (especially the fine forms of *Fuchsia magellanica*) are not put out by being used as support.

Small scallop-edged leaves, slightly mottled with paler green, are attractive all summer, but in autumn, when nature seems to be stage-managing a final glorious show before the great leaf-fall, these little leaves tinted with scarlet and bronze also add sparks of warmth, complementing the cool, innocent-eyed flowers.

Throughout October I keep a jam pot beside my wellington boots to remind me to collect the seed, as it breeds true. About twice a week I visit my plants to look for the long bill-shaped seed heads which are just turning brown. If I am too late the 'bill' will have split, catapulting the hard seeds which are attached to its base. Any soil which does not dry out, in sun, or shade, will suit this plant.

Geranium wallichianum 'Buxton's Variety'

Physostegia virginiana

The Obedient Plant

The physostegias belong to the Labiate family; they all have tubular flowers with conspicuous frilly lips. They are found wild in damp places in the east-central United States and Canada. In gardens they thrive in almost any soil that does not dry out, preferably in sun. They can be grown from seed, or plants can be divided and replanted in autumn or spring. Their vivid spires of flower make useful accents and contrast of form among low-growing or cushion-shaped plants.

Physostegia virginiana 'Vivid' flowers from late September well into November, making a bright patch of fresh colour on the edge of a damp but sunny border. Running shoots send many slender stems ($1-1\frac{1}{2}$ ft.) alternately set with pairs of narrow, fine-toothed leaves. Tapering spires, sometimes branched, of close set, narrow tubular flowers make a glowing display for weeks on end. Look carefully and you will see that each head consists of four rows of densely-packed flowers, the same colour as the colchicums nearby, a bright rosy-purple. Starting from the bottom the flowers slowly open, leaving behind crowded tiers of green calyces, with no faded flowers to look untidy.

Why the Obedient Plant? Because if you pick a stem you will find the individual flowers stand out from the stem on hinged 'brackets'. You can move them and they will stay put to face another way. Why ever was such a complicated mechanism evolved?

There is a form called *P. v.* 'Summer Snow' which has white flowers in August, on stems $2\frac{1}{2}-3$ ft. tall. The upturned spires of green calyces left behind when the flowers have dropped make an interesting shape for those who love to make green flower arrangements.

Physostegia virginiana speciosa is a variety with larger and more coarsely toothed leaves. 'Rose Bouquet' is a form of this and with its tall ($2\frac{1}{2}-3$ ft.) spires of lilac-pink flowers it makes a long-lasting display from high summer till September. These plants can be grown from seed or cuttings, or plants can easily be divided and replanted in refreshed soil in autumn or spring.

Cimicifugas

There are a number of different cimicifugas. Some have been called Bug-bane, because the scent of their leaves was thought to drive away bugs. The leaves of *Cimicifuga simplex* 'White Pearl' have no smell that I can detect, and fortunately I have no bugs to repel. These are not the easiest of plants to grow in dry districts. They need deep moist soil, and some protection from strong sunlight for their handsome, finely cut leaves which suffer from sunscorch. By mid October a stately array of tall, almost bare branching wands stand above the basal leaves, topped with elegant spires of round, pale green buds. These slowly open to become a bottlebrush of tiny, fluffy white flowers. The pure ice-white effect is prolonged over several weeks by side branches which open when the terminal spires have faded. Quick to follow are light green seed heads, making another attractive feature well into November.

The form called *C. s.* 'Elstead' is similar but has thin stems stained purple, as are the small round buds which give a hint of warmth to the ivory-white flowers. Although standing up to 4 ft. tall these plants need no staking and take up little room. Their freshness is unexpected so late in the season. A north-facing situation, with a dark background suits them well.

Cimicifuga cordifolia has much less finely cut leaves, not unlike those of a Japanese Anemone, and makes a good background plant among late summer flowering perennials with its tall (5 ft.) stems carrying stiffly held spires of creamy-green flowers.

Cimicifuga simplex ramosa produces a long succession of pure white flowers throughout October, good with the deep rich lavender-blue of *Aconitum carmichaelii*.

A form known as 'Atropurpurea' is still a rarity in this country, but it is perhaps the finest of all this handsome family. The large, broadly cut leaves are heavily stained purple, so too are the stiff, slender, branching stems which stand over 6 ft. high. The unopened buds are tinted the same deep shade while the pure white flowers, last of all the cimicifugas to open, show pink-tinted stamens. Unexpected, but never forgotten, is the exquisite perfume of this aristocratic plant.

All cimicifugas can be grown from seed, or division of roots throughout the dormant season. Being rather slow to increase they are not over-abundant, but are well worth waiting for.

Cimicifuga simplex

Aster lateriflorus 'Horizontalis'

A Strange Michaelmas Daisy

Few flowers remain perfect for long, fewer still become more handsome as weeks go by. There is an unusual Michaelmas Daisy which does exactly that. It is called *Aster lateriflorus* 'Horizontalis' and I cannot think why it should be unusual. At the end of the first week of November, after several light frosts and days of blustering gales, which we can always expect at this time of year, my bushy little plants are smothered with flowers, with scarcely an untidy one among them. They are a delight, in form and colour.

Each plant sends up several stems about 2 ft. high. Each stiffly upright stem is furnished with long horizontal branches which subdivide again, producing a wide triangular head set with tiny dark green leaves. About the end of September the flowers begin to open, small and pale, so insignificant you might well think there was every good reason not to grow this plant. But wait; as the weeks go by, as colour is blown from the garden and the nights grow colder, these little green bushes become transformed; thickly starred with flowers which have opened wide their tiny, glistening white petals to make way for the slowly expanding cushions of deep rosy-mauve fluff which fill their centres. They hold the colour and freshness as all the thousands of flowers on one plant gradually open. I have planted three plants in a group which together make a dense mass of blossom, 5 ft. across.

So firm and compact are the interlaced branches that some people, seeing this plant for the first time imagine it is a shrub. In fact I have seen it grown as a seasonal hedging plant. At Great Dixter, Christopher Lloyd has used it in a little courtyard which is dominated by a 'Parliament of Peacocks' mounted on tall pedestals of clipped yew. Edging the paved paths between these 'architectural' features, and providing just the right contrast, I saw little hedges made of this untypical Michaelmas Daisy. Weak winter sunlight gilded their lace-like sprays, still studded with tiny cushions of pale fluff; a hoar frost would have made the scene magical. By the time the old stems are cut down in spring fresh young shoots already mark the border's edge.

This aster likes an open situation in retentive soil, and can be propagated by cuttings or division.

Ornamental Vines

Still glowing with warm colour in my garden are several ornamental vines. The first is *Vitis vinifera* 'Purpurea'. Throughout the summer the young leaves have a downy texture which gives them a pale silvery look, but as they expand the veins become purple, and a claret-tinted flush spreads over the face of mature leaves. This contrast of young and mature foliage all summer gives a lightness that is attractive. From September the colour deepens overall; by November the long trailing vines are still heavy with rich purple-coloured leaves, glowing like wine when lit by late autumn sunlight. Clusters of grapes, black and bloomy, are handsome but too sour for most tastes.

My second vine is *V. coignetiae*, one of the most spectacular climbers we can grow. Huge, heart-shaped leaves, green all summer, are much veined and crinkled; the texture of embossed leather. As contrast their backs remain light copper coloured, covered with fine felt. As the first chills of autumn creep in, it is as though a match were put to the great ropes of leaves which may cascade from a wall, or tumble from the top of a tall tree. Shades of crimson, scarlet and yellow burn as bright as the embers of autumn bonfires.

Very different is *Ampelopsis brevipedunculata* which also belongs to the vine family. If it is planted against a south-facing wall, and then blessed with a fine hot summer you may, in October, have the thrill of watching the extraordinary mixture of colour produced by its small, bead-like, round fruits. Slowly maturing over several weeks they turn from purple to dark blue and finally are an unbelievable turquoise, speckled like a bird's egg. They are produced on lateral shoots which cascade from the wall and are held in clusters above delicate leaves which, by November have become clear lemon-yellow. The combination is unforgettable.

Vines should be planted when dormant, in very well-prepared soil. Once they have made strong roots and a woody base they will make yards of growth throughout the summer. They should be pruned in winter, cutting the past season's shoots back to two or three strong buds close to the main framework.

Vitis vinifera 'Purpurea'

Physalis franchetii

Chinese Lanterns

My Chinese Lanterns, ignored for the whole of the summer, illuminate their patch for months in autumn, lasting well into winter. They seem to be considered old-fashioned, and are not very popular at the moment for I rarely see them in gardens. Perhaps it is due to their tendency to wander from their allotted space, and the fact that their stems are rather floppy. But, when their inflated, pointed seed pods have ripened to an almost savage orange, I find the floppiness of the stems becomes an advantage, making them more graceful to arrange in a narrow necked jar with a few straw-coloured grasses, or a pod or two of the orange-berried *Iris foetidissima*.

Physalis franchetii belongs to the same family as the potato and tomato. In midsummer its small cream-coloured flowers are rather hidden along the leafy stems, but many flower arrangers must be enchanted by their 'lanterns' long before they have been set alight, when they are well formed but still green. Some arrangers carefully tear open each ripened papery case to make four-petalled 'flowers', and then the small tomato-like fruit is seen inside. These are not poisonous, but I do not find them very appetising to eat.

The best time to cut the stems for winter is on a warm, dry day when most of the lanterns are rich orange-red. Pick off any tattered remains of leaves and hang the stems up to dry in a warm airy place.

Sometimes, in dead of winter, I discover a last remaining stem sheltering in the low, scrubby tangle of an old-fashioned rose (these two wanderers seem to associate well together) and find a few perfect lanterns, all colour gone, just the fretted veins remaining; inside, the still orange fruit rolls around like an imprisoned jewel inside a filigree container.

They grow in almost any soil, but prefer not to be dried out in midsummer. Like all plants they reward you if you feed them occasionally with additional humus. They are least nuisance and most appreciated when planted among low shrubs. They need sunlight to produce good 'lanterns' so do not bury them where it is too dark.

Rooted pieces can be planted any time between autumn and spring, or they can be grown from seed.

Snowberries

When I was a child I was regularly disappointed by a thicket of suckering shrubs growing in a dim corner of my parents' garden. Scattered here and there among the twiggy branches and small leaden-green leaves were large, round, white berries, about the size of marbles. If only, I thought, there was more than one berry to the square foot of leafage, what an exciting shrub this would be. Now, much older, and a little more experienced, I am still not certain whether these bushes were *Symphoricarpos albus*, or *S. rivularis*, both of which are called 'Snowberry', both of which should stay tucked well away as undergrowth for pheasant cover in woodland.

There are several other species, including *S. orbiculatus* which makes a pleasantly shaped low spreading shrub carrying clusters of rather too small purplish-rose berries.

Marriages have been arranged between these less than exciting shrubs which have produced much improved hybrids, most welcome in the autumn garden. One of the best is *S.* 'Mother of Pearl'. It makes a small dense bush about 3–4 ft. high and across, its branches thickly clustered with marble-sized berries which are flushed clover-pink on top where the sun touches them, but white beneath. For flower arrangers these branches are a delight, associating well with sprays of heather or small-flowered chrysanthemums. To obtain the best shaped sprays of berry prune out old twiggy pieces, and reduce some of the current year's fruiting branches, so that each year there is room and vigour to make straight young stems. This shrub barely suckers at all, but can be grown from hardwood cuttings when the leaves have fallen.

Symphoricarpos 'White Hedge' makes a small shrub of strong upright growth, freely producing small white berries in erect clusters. Another form, valued both by flower arrangers and gardeners who may be looking for a shrub with interesting leaves, is *S. orbiculatus* 'Variegatus'. It does not sucker, but makes a very pretty shrub, its small, neat, pale green leaves edged with yellow, very useful to lighten up a dull border (many flowering shrubs are dreary when not in flower). I did not think this shrub set berries, but one winter, when the leaves had dropped, I was amazed to see thin, wiry stems set with small clusters of seed-pearl sized berries, soft mauve in colour.

Symphoricarposes are not fussy about soil, but are less likely to fruit abundantly in thoroughly starved conditions. They can be used to form hedges and will grow in sun or shade, tolerating roots and drip from large trees.

Symphoricarpos 'Mother of Pearl'

Haplopappus coronopifolius

Haplopappus coronopifolius

Haplopappus coronopifolius is not a name that slips easily off the tongue, which is a pity because it might be as popular as *Arabis* if people felt they could dare to pronounce it. It has three endearing habits. It will hang over a wall, or sprawl on to a piece of paving where it softens the hard edge. It is evergreen, so makes a good looking feature all the year round, and it flowers from mid summer onwards. At the end of November it still carries fresh flowers, and buds continue into December if the weather remains mild. Small orange daisies, about one inch across, are sprinkled over a background of narrow, dark green leaves which furnish a low hummock of woody stems. It is not a dazzling plant, but neat and tidy, embroidered with daisies for months on end. Because its leaves are small and almost leathery in texture this plant will tolerate dry conditions in full sun. But where the soil is poor sand or gravel it would help if you dug in some well-rotted compost to give it a good start.

Originally I had a plant which made a fine feature on the corner of a raised bed where it draped itself to the ground, masking the hard edge. After several years it was past its best so I replaced it with a young plant, but elsewhere another mature specimen, several feet across, sprawls beside a shallow flight of steps where its dark evergreen leaves contrast well with low carpets of golden-leafed thyme, silvery-blue acaenas, and white woolly mounds of santolinas. Good to look at from the comfort of a warm room, these plants create a living carpet, much more heartening in winter than yards of bare mud where leaf-losing perennials have retreated underground.

If *Haplopappus* sounds attractive but too large for your situation you can always trim it in spring together with bush thymes and any other companions which might well be rejuvenated by well considered pruning. It is not a rampant plant, but several planted together can provide good ground cover where it is needed.

Cuttings or rooted pieces are the usual means of propagation. Sometimes seen listed as *H. lyallii* this name is probably synonymous.

An Evergreen Iris

Iris foetidissima 'Citrina' is one of the plants I would keep if my gardening was reduced to ten plants. Whether you have a tiny backyard or several acres, this plant catches the eye, winter and summer. Most people think of irises as having splendid, almost orchid-like flowers. This iris produces modest flowers of a soft buttery-yellow, delicately veined with brown, that are rather small for the size of the plant. By November large fat seed pods have been formed, so heavy that they lean out from among the green blade-like leaves. Gradually they split open into three parts, each section of pod curved backwards and crinkled to show a double row of shining orange seeds, big as young peas. They cling to the crinkled cream-lined pods for some time and are a bright contrast above the autumn leaf-litter.

They last well if picked and placed, without water, in a jug on some high shelf. But what I value most are the long evergreen leaves, of a rich shining green. They make a fine arching clump of living colour which draws the eye all winter, providing a dignified background for something more ephemeral in summer.

From time to time you need to cut out, or pull out, the old and untidy leaves to make way for the new ones. Occasionally old plants are better scrapped, to be replaced by fresh young seedlings which can usually be found nearby. They will grow almost anywhere, except in waterlogged soil. They thrive in dry shade so are invaluable under trees and shrubs, or in dim town gardens where their arching clumps of fresh evergreen leaves catch the light and make just the right contrast for round-leafed plants such as bergenias.

This plant is, I think, a more worthy garden plant than the ordinary *I. foetidissima* which is a native plant still to be found growing wild in some counties on the edges of woods or hedgerows, but it has smaller flowers of a rather drab shade of blue, and less impressive seed pods.

Iris foetidissima 'Variegata' is much appreciated by both gardeners and flower arrangers. It seldom flowers, so division is the only means of propagation. Some time in late February or early March is the best time to do this. Then you will see that new, sturdy white roots are already emerging from the base of the individual fans. These fans can easily be prised, or carefully cut apart, the leaves and old roots reduced slightly and the pieces replanted. They take time to recover, but by late summer they will have made two or three fans of beautiful cream and green striped leaves, very effective in the winter garden.

Iris foetidissima 'Citrina'

Sedum 'Autumn Joy'

Sedum 'Autumn Joy'

I love plants which contribute to the design of the garden for weeks on end. *Sedum* 'Autumn Joy' provides colour and interest literally for months. Next year's shoots already formed sit as tightly clustered buds just at soil level. Next spring they will quickly develop rosettes of jade-green leaves, which some people, not unreasonably, call Ice Plants. Certainly the succulent leaves have a pale icy appearance, a smooth brittle texture. Throughout the summer they make effective contrast with other flowering plants. By August their flower buds are packed into large flat heads, the same colour as the leaves. Slowly a coral tinge seeps into the curious clustered buds. By the end of September they are old-brick red. In the latter days of November, although the colour has darkened to a rich mahogany-red they light up the grey garden, catching my eye as I look up from my writing. Finally the red will drain away and the dry heads will become warm chestnut brown standing firm until they are cut down.

Sedum 'Autumn Joy' is a hybrid, probably with *S. spectabile* as a parent. *S. spectabile* makes a similar shaped plant but its little starry flowers are soft mauve-pink. Sometimes it is a wishy-washy colour but there is a good form called 'Brilliant' which is lovely but does not retain its colour after October. These are the sedums which attract Peacock and Admiral butterflies in late summer. Curiously *S.* 'Autumn Joy' is never visited by butterflies, but it is crowded with honey bees.

These large sedums flourish in full sun, in well-drained, even poor, sandy or stony soil. But they produce finer and larger heads of flower if there is a little humus in the soil, and if occasionally they are divided in spring.

There are many other members of this large and tolerant family which I should hate to be without. In gardens which suffer from drought they are a blessing with their healthy-looking foliage, and many produce sheets of starry blossoms. Some form carpets of tiny succulent rosettes which drop off and root in small crevices, others have handsomely variegated leaves, while many of the alpine species remain to furnish the garden in winter.

Schizostylis, the Kaffir Lily

Tall-stemmed and elegant, lovely to pick from September almost until Christmas, these exotic flowers from South Africa are an unexpected pleasure to find in cold foggy November gardens. During the growing season they must have plenty of sun and warmth but they also need moisture during the summer months to produce the nice fat shoots which will elongate into flower spikes in autumn. Above running clumps of light green, blade-shaped leaves stand bare slender stems (2–2½ ft.) topped with spires of pointed buds. These slowly open from the base upwards, and while a sudden sharp frost will reduce the translucent crimson petals to mush it will not harm the buds which continue to open well into December.

Schizostylis coccinea is sometimes described as looking like a small gladiolus; both belong to the Iris family, but the flower shape reminds me more of the true autumn crocuses which are still flowering in the garden. Six petals open to form a perfect shallow, bowl-shaped flower of glistening silky texture. *S. c.* 'Major' has larger and finer flowers of light luminous red.

There are several named pink forms. 'Sunrise' was introduced by the Plantsmen and has large rose-pink flowers. 'November Cheer' is still in splendid form late in the year and was introduced by Alan Bloom. 'Viscountess Byng' is one of the oldest and best known pink forms but it has never grown successfully in my garden, only a few miles away from the garden of its namesake where I gather it did no better. Drought and drying winds are largely to blame. Schizostylises are probably most successful in the warm and moist counties of south west England where they make a fine show of flower throughout the autumn, but in colder counties, especially in heavy soils, their flower buds may often be produced too late.

In fertile soil and full sun these plants increase well making dense mats of searching roots and shoots. It is best to divide them every few years in the spring, setting out the best pieces in refreshed soil. A mulch of straw or bracken over the roots is a wise precaution in winter, especially in very cold districts, but remember to remove most of it in spring to allow the grassy shoots to grow through. Cold heavy soils need to be lightened with sand or grit to encourage them to increase and flower consistently.

Schizostylis coccinea 'Major' and *S.c.* 'Sunrise'

Cortaderia selloana 'Pumila'

Pampas Grass

Battered and bedraggled by wind and rain, discoloured by car fumes or polluted air, it is not surprising that some people shudder when you suggest using Pampas Grass as a centre of interest in the autumn garden. But in the country, with space and clean air around them, I think they are a noble sight. In Chile they grow wild alongside stream beds, sometimes with gigantic stands of *Chusquea couleou*, a most handsome bamboo, seldom seen in British gardens, with canes usually 6–10 ft, but can grow up to 27 ft.

Good and bad forms are seen in gardens. Grown from seed you may get some rather poor skinny flower heads, certainly not worth the space. Two selected and named forms I especially like are *Cortaderia selloana* 'Pumila' and *C. s.* 'Sunningdale Silver'. 'Pumila' means dwarf, but do not let that mislead you. This Pampas Grass makes dense clumps of shorter, arching foliage, but in good deep soil the flower stems stand 5–6 ft. The flower heads are also dense, with colour and texture reminiscent of Arran wool, a soft creamy-beige. They look best when viewed with the sun behind you, planted perhaps at the end of a walk.

My favourite is *C. s.* 'Sunningdale Silver', whose drooping plumes are much more open and delicate in shape. Planted by the waterside they tower 8–10 ft. tall, their silvery-white pennants gleaming among the rich copper and gold of autumn-tinted trees and shrubs which form a frame around them.

There are other named forms of *C. selloana* which I have not grown. 'Monstrosa' has immense creamy-white plumes. 'Rendatleri' is another giant with pink-tinted plumes. I am not sure that I like pink Pampas Grass. In those I have seen the colour tends to be a dark purplish shade staining the silvery whiteness of the flowers, and can, wrongly placed in bad light, look dingy.

Cortaderia selloana 'Aureo-lineata' is possibly a form now sold as 'Goldband'. It is variegated with yellow and pale green striped leaves which continue to make a lovely feature in the garden in mild winters, but can be damaged by prolonged and hard frost.

Pampas Grass grows well in open situations in any retentive soil. It should be divided only in spring, and then nursed in containers and sheltered until new roots are formed.

Abelia × grandiflora

This shrub has so many good qualities that I am compelled to write about it, although it is slightly tender and may not succeed in very cold districts. But provided it is shielded from north-east wind-frosts and grown in hungry gravel rather than a heavy wet soil it seems to do very well. It must surely be one of the best shrubs for a south or west wall where it makes a light graceful shape covered with small, oval, shining leaves which are warmly tinted bronze. Throughout the late summer and autumn it is smothered with a succession of pale pink, flushed, tubular flowers. As these drop they leave behind starry petalled bracts which gradually become deep coral, and enhance the pale delicacy of the fresh flowers still to open. By December, when a few flowers may still be found if we have had a mild spell, the whole bush is glowing with these packed terminal clusters of bracts, almost smothering the leaves, which look as though they too reflected the warm colour. For late autumn and early winter flower arrangements little sprigs of this shrub are a joy. A light trim in the spring to remove any winter damage or worn out woody pieces will keep the shrub tidy and ensure a good supply of young fresh branches.

Abelia schumannii makes a smaller, more delicate shrub with lilac tinted flowers. It needs the protection of a warm wall and can be damaged in very severe winters, but in warmer counties I imagine it might do very well.

Abeliophyllum distichum, not commonly seen, is not related at all; its name means that it has leaves like *Abelia*. I have these two shrubs growing near each other, against a sheltered wall. In winter the *Abeliophyllum* is leafless, a graceful shape made of many slender curving branches closely set with small, dark purple buds. In January a few sprays brought into the house will open small, pure white flowers to make the prettiest spring-like decoration for the table. The warmth of the room also brings out a faintly musky perfume.

This is a slow-growing shrub so patience is needed before you can fill large vases. In the garden the flowers will open in February during mild spells and, provided they are not suddenly burned brown by frost, will make a delightful and unexpected display. Left to open naturally in the garden the opening buds are tinted salmon-pink, of which there was no sign on the forced branches in winter.

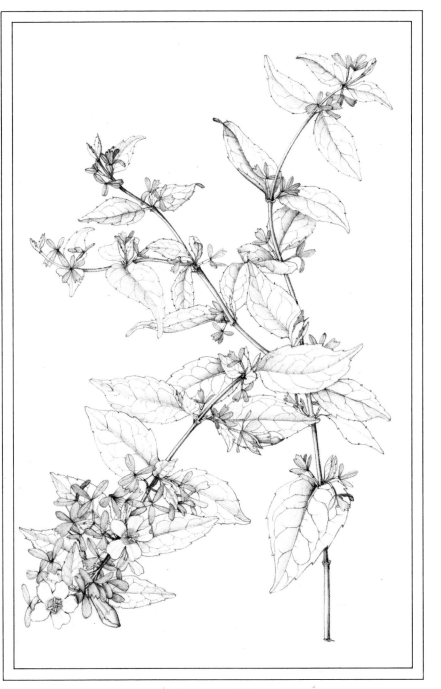

Abelia × grandiflora

Arum italicum 'Pictum'

A Hardy Arum

As the garden retreats into the dark depths of winter few plants, except evergreens, remain fresh and unharmed. Most are resting, waiting for the spring. But for *Arum italicum* 'Pictum' (of gardens) the new year commences in October when its leaves, like rolled cigars, start to push through the damp soil. Slowly they unfold and continue to grow throughout the winter.

This hardy *Arum* is one of the aristocrats of all foliage plants, isolated in the winter garden. The beautiful leaves held upright on firm stalks are long and narrowly spear shaped with curving edges. The base colour is dark, satin-textured green over which is laid a marbled pattern in shades of cream and green. The leaves come in many sizes. You can find small ones to put with the first snowdrops, something larger for the early daffodils, until, by May, you can find leaves big enough to put with the large white arum lilies used for Easter decorations. Their own flowers are transparent palest green, hidden among the leaves in May. You may not even notice them. By the end of June every trace of plant has vanished. In September stems of juicy scarlet berries appear unexpectedly through the bare soil. They are poisonous to humans, so warn the children.

They are easy to grow in shady conditions provided you first dig a large hole, at least the size of a bucket, fill it with well-rotted vegetable waste, stir it up thoroughly with the soil and then plant one or two tubers when dormant from July to September, or from autumn to spring if container grown.

If you have a friend who could supply you with berries it is worthwhile growing new plants from seed, but you must be prepared for a long wait before you will see full-sized leaves. The seeds sometimes lie in the soil twelve months before they germinate and then the newly emerged seedlings look nothing like their parents. They are small, scarcely so large as a teaspoon, plain green in colour, on stalks not much more than one inch high. The next year they may look much the same, perhaps a little larger, but the third year you will have a properly shaped leaf showing a faintly marbled effect. Each following year the leaves will be larger, more numerous, and strongly marked.

An old tuber may be as large as the ball of your thumb. After several years one tuber will have increased to form a clump of varying sizes. Attached to the larger tubers are tiny pea-sized babies. Like the seeds, these take several years before they are big enough to produce large well-marked leaves, and stems of brilliant berries.

Bergenias

These are some of my favourite plants. In winter their large clusters of evergreen leaves relieve the boredom of bare soil, while in summer they produce handsome flowers. More important their large bold leaves create a calming effect among a froth of fussy foliaged plants.

Bergenia cordifolia 'Purpurea' has large, rounded leaves of leathery texture, strongly veined and slightly puckered, arranged in large rosettes which make a handsome effect on the edge of a border. With the first touch of frost the top sides become suffused with red, producing a polished bronze effect while their backs have a lighter almost crimson glow.

Bergenia crassifolia 'Autumn Red' has narrower more upright leaves which become even more brilliantly tinted. I was brought up with *B.* × *schmidtii*, and I suspect that many gardens still grow only this form of *Bergenia*. Its disadvantage is that its lovely pink flowers, which are the first to open, are too often reduced to pulp by spring frost, and its leaves never change colour in winter. Both *B. cordifolia* and *B. crassifolia* flower later, on tall rhubarb-red stalks.

There are many other bergenias. Not all colour well in winter but one which turns the deepest tone of all, at the first touch of cold in November, almost the colour of raw liver backed with thrilling carmine-pink is *B. purpurascens*. Its narrow leaves are held erect like the ears of a hare and the new leaves remain dark green all summer. The colour and form of its flowers are also distinctive—narrow, drooping heads of coral-red, bell-shaped flowers on tall slender reddish stems.

There are other species worth growing, while many hybrids give collectors almost as great a chance for one-upmanship as collectors of hostas. Among some of the best is *B.* 'Abendglut' (Evening Glow) which makes very neat rosettes of crinkled leaves darkly shaded with maroon and crimson in winter, brilliantly lit in spring with semi-double flowers of a particularly vivid cherry-pink. *B.* 'Silberlicht' has large heads of white flowers which become tinted shell-pink as they mature, but its leaves scarcely change colour in winter.

New names include 'Baby Doll' and 'Opal' both of which have large shell-pink flowers, while there are many good hybrids being introduced which consistently produce good winter colour. Among them is a seedling bred by Eric Smith which I consider the very best, and have called it after him.

These plants will grow in any soil, in sun or shade, but the best winter colour develops when they are grown in full exposure, in not too well-enriched soil.

Bergenia crassifolia 'Autumn Red'

Skimmia japonica

Skimmia japonica

Everyone loves to see red berries at Christmastime; they are so heart-warming, a perfect contrast to shining evergreen leaves. Not everyone has room to grow a holly tree, and some years no berries are set and the trees look dark, unlit, like empty lamps.

Every autumn my *Skimmia* bushes are loaded with shining clusters of red berries, and are still fresh as can be on Christmas Day. *S. japonica* makes an ideal shrub for a small garden. It is low and rounded into a neat comfortable shape, covered with rosettes of smooth evergreen leaves. It looks well placed on the edge of a border, or used to back a patio where you can see the welcome colour from the house. The berries remain bright for months, totally ignored by birds. In fact they remain till the next season's fruit is formed.

There is one problem: you need male and female plants to ensure a good crop. Fortunately, to help identify them there is a male clone called *S. j.* 'Rubella'. It has handsome clusters of small maroon-red buds which remain good looking all winter, opening to small creamy flowers in spring. For a female you must obtain a plant from a nursery which has taken cuttings from the right bush (that is the one which fruits) and has kept them labelled! Or you can grow them from berries, and wait until several plants mature together, when you should see that you have one of each sex.

I have several bushes grown from seed which show slight variations. Some bushes have much paler leaves which almost look as though they were sun bleached, yet they are growing beside another which has perfectly normal rich green leaves.

Some of my male plants have larger leaves, and larger trusses of flower than the selected form 'Rubella', but the buds are not so richly coloured.

Skimmia japonica 'Fragrans' is a free-flowing male clone with dense panicles of white flowers, scented like Lily-of-the-Valley. Crushed in the hand the leaves of *Skimmia* give off a sweet spicey perfume.

All forms can be grown in any reasonably fertile soil, in sun or part shade. They can be planted any time from autumn until spring.

Fatsia japonica

Some people confuse this shrub both with the Castor Oil Plant and the Fig. *Ricinus communis*, the Castor Oil Plant, does have similar shaped leaves but it is half-hardy and herbaceous, usually used as a handsome feature among summer annuals. Fig leaves are somewhat similar, but neither so handsome nor evergreen.

Fatsia japonica has large, shining evergreen leaves whose rounded shapes are deeply divided to form long pointed lobes or fingers. They are held well out from the main stout stems on long stiff stalks. Fatsia is related to ivy, and in early winter carries attractive sprays of pale cream-coloured flowers, very like the green clusters of flower produced on the fruiting stems of ivy. These pallid balls of flower and their cream stems make a startling contrast above the layers of polished dark green leaves. In mild districts, with only light frosts, clusters of black berries will follow which are both handsome and useful, to raise new plants from seed. But in my garden they are more often shrivelled by hard frost. However, the foliage is seldom damaged. It forms one of the most distinctive evergreen shrubs, ideal to plant in shade as an imposing feature beneath a building or wall.

If it grows too large you can thin out some of the stout stems from the base, and shorten others. The new stems will carry larger leaves, given more light and air. There is a form with variegated leaves, *F. j.* 'Variegata', but it is more susceptible to frost damage. The lobed leaves are bordered with white at the tips.

If you cannot obtain seed, *F. japonica* can be grown from cuttings. Take tip shoots in August, about 10–12 inches long. Reduce the leaves to the top two or three, and pot each cutting separately, dropping sharp sand around the base and stem of each cutting. Place the pots under a mist propagator with bottom heat which helps them to root quite quickly. Without such aids you could try a closed case—a box with a glass lid, placed in a warm greenhouse would do. When rooted, over-winter the young plants in a frost-free greenhouse, or bring them indoors where they do well as house plants.

The plant called × *Fatshedera lizei*, which is said to be a cross between *Fatsia* and Irish Ivy (*Hedera helix* 'Hibernica'), makes a good feature plant tumbling down a bank or trained in a tub for a conservatory. It has rather lax woody stems and clusters of leaves smaller that *Fatsia*, but boldly shaped. × *Fatshedera lizei* 'Variegata' has grey-green leaves with irregular creamy-white margins.

Fatsia japonica

Ilex × *altaclarensis* 'Golden King'

A Bunch of Hollies

If your acquaintance with Holly is confined to the few sprigs you buy from a street barrow, to tuck behind the pictures for Christmas decoration, then you might be in for a surprise, and ultimately a treat, if you studied Hillier's *Manual of Trees and Shrubs* where seven pages are taken describing many different species and cultivars. Some are familiar in gardens and parks, others are much less well-known.

I am always looking for good evergreens to make a background or framework for the garden in winter. Too many conifers can be monotonous, and not everyone has the soil or climate for rhododendrons. Hollies are easily grown in most soils. They add style and character to garden design and can be kept in good shape by pruning.

Ilex aquifolium, the Common Holly, is a native in Britain extending from Europe to China. Cultivated since ancient times there are now many beautiful cultivars selected for their variously shaped and coloured leaves.

Most of us hope to see berries on our holly. One of the best to produce regular crops of large, bright red fruits is *I. a.* 'J. C. van Tol', with oval glossy leaves which are without too many prickles. Try to plant your tree so that you will look at it with the sun shining on the berries. I planted mine on my west-facing boundary so unless I am about fairly early in the morning I have to walk along my neighbouring farmer's boundary to see the crowded clusters of fruit lit up by winter sunset.

I particularly like holly with yellow berries. I have one grown from a cutting, which is probably *I. a.* 'Bacciflava' ('Fructuluteo'). Its long graceful branches are closely set with yellow berries which are not raided by birds until all the red ones have gone.

Ilex aquifolium 'Angustifolia' is very distinguished. I sometimes use it as a slim vertical, in place of the upright Juniper (*Juniperus communis* 'Hibernica'). It has pretty dark green leaves, the perfect holly shape, but the largest is scarcely an inch long—ideal for decorating the base of a Christmas cake.

There are many different forms of holly with variegated leaves. For the large garden *I.* × *altaclarensis* 'Golden King' is magnificent with large, broad, almost spineless leaves, richly margined with creamy-yellow. For confined spaces the Golden Hedgehog Holly, *I. aquifolium* 'Ferox Aurea' is slow growing, with small, very undulated, very prickly leaves with pale butter-yellow centres.

Colour from Stems

Few people have gardens large enough to take a mature Weeping Willow, which must be allowed to achieve full height and spread to show off its graceful and noble proportions. But there are several other willows which need not take up much room, and which look very attractive on a corner of damp land, or just in heavy soil that does not dry out. I am thinking particularly of willows and dogwoods with coloured stems which look so good in winter. Among the different kinds can be found stems which may be yellow, polished purple-black, bloom-coated purple, and brilliant orange-red.

Salix alba 'Chermesina', or 'Britzensis' as we used to call it, is the Scarlet Willow, and the most outstanding. It is at its best in winter when sunlight strikes the polished stems forming a trellis through which perhaps you may view the frozen surface of water beyond. Or better still, when snow has fallen, there is brilliant contrast between orange-red stems emerging from the white quilt below, and blue sky above.

If left to itself this willow would make a large, densely twiggy thicket of a bush, or small tree, when the growth is less vigorous, and the colour not so bright. If you allow it to make a short trunk, and then cut it hard, leaving just a small framework of branches, new vigorous stems will shoot up several feet in one season, looking as though they were varnished in vivid orange-scarlet paint. I prune mine every second year, sometime in early spring before the leaf buds have burst.

The Dogwood family also produces shrubs with handsome, coloured stems in winter. *Cornus alba* is the red barked dogwood which will grow in wet or dry soils forming thickets 8 or 9 ft. high. There are several good forms. *C. a.* 'Sibirica' has the most brilliant crimson shoots. Its leaves colour well in autumn, and its terminal clusters of small white berries are tinted with blue. *C. a.* 'Spaethii' has not quite such brilliant winter colour but it is among the most beautiful of summer foliage shrubs, with large oval leaves conspicuously variegated with gold.

Cornus stolonifera 'Flaviramea' looks particularly good when its cool olive green shoots are reflected in still dark water.

These dogwoods should be pruned every other year, in March.

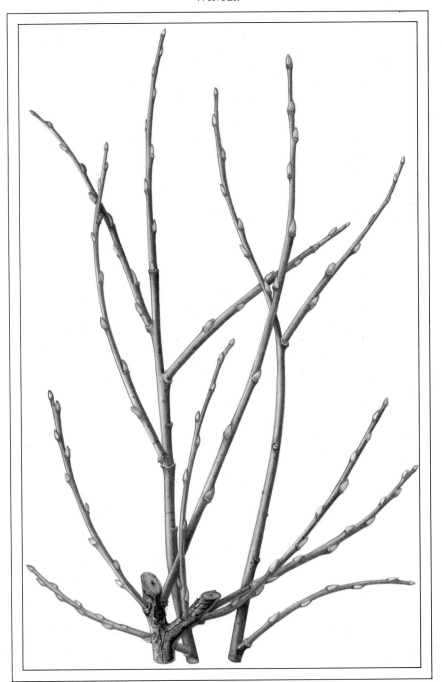

Salix alba 'Chermesina'

INDEX

Numbers printed in bold indicate illustrations